SCHOOLBOY
SCIENCE
REMEMBERED

SCHOOLBOY
SCIENCE
REMEMBERED

by

Dr Keith Souter

Illustrations by Andrew James

First published in Great Britain in 2011 by
Remember When
an imprint of
Pen & Sword Books Ltd
47 Church Street
Barnsley
South Yorkshire
S70 2AS

ISBN 978 1 84468 097 9

A CIP catalogue record for this book is
available from the British Library

Typeset in Sabon by
Phoenix Typesetting, Auldgirth, Dumfriesshire

Printed and bound in England by
CPI UK

Pen & Sword Books Ltd incorporates the Imprints of Pen & Sword Aviation,
Pen & Sword Maritime, Pen & Sword Military, Wharncliffe Local History, Pen
& Sword Select, Pen & Sword Military Classics and Leo Cooper.

For a complete list of Pen & Sword titles please contact
PEN & SWORD BOOKS LIMITED
47 Church Street, Barnsley, South Yorkshire, S70 2AS, England
E-mail: enquiries@pen-and-sword.co.uk
Website: www.pen-and-sword.co.uk

CONTENTS

ACKNOWLEDGEMENTS

First and foremost I want to thank Sir Patrick Moore for being such an inspirational figure in astronomy and a role model for so many people, myself included, whose interests in science were sparked off by watching him present *The Sky at Night.*

I also have to thank all of the science teachers that I have known along the way, but most especially to Prang, who spurred my interest in chemistry. I even forgive him for not showing me how to make stink bombs all those years ago.

Andrew James, my talented illustrator, has been a pleasure to work with. He deftly turned my ideas and crude sketches into first-rate pieces of artwork. They are so good and reflect the experiments that I was doing that I suspect he had a hidden camera somewhere in my kitchen and bathroom.

Fiona Shoop was the commissioning editor at Pen & Sword who actually came up with the idea of the book. I am grateful to her for the opportunity of delving back through my old school notebooks and my even older memory on this nostalgic trip through schoolboy science. She was also extremely helpful in advising me about where and how to obtain illustrations and photographs, and how to avoid pitfalls over copyright material. Thank you, Fiona.

Lisa Hooson has been helpful in guiding me through the production process and Jill Morris, my editor at Pen & Sword, has skilfully shaped the book into the finished product.

Along the way I have been in contact with many wonderful folk who have helped me find pictures to go alongside Andrew James's splendid drawings. So thank you to:

The Mary Evans Picture Library for the front cover photograph.

The Whipple Museum of the History of Science, University of Cambridge for the portrait of Sir Isaac Newton.

Lance S Borman at the Borden Radio Company, for his help with building a crystal set.

Vic Whittle, the extremely knowledgeable owner of British Comics website, (http://www.britishcomics.20m.com/home.htm) was fantastic in helping me track down the serial about Cat's Whiskers Kelly in *The Hotspur*. I bow to his encyclopaedic knowledge of British comics.

Bill McLoughlin at the Syndication Department at DC Thomson in Dundee was equally generous in obtaining the actual camera ready pages from the hallowed comic *The Hotspur*, and in giving me permission to use the very first serial.

Delphine Maubert at MOULINSART in Brussels for permission to use the picture of Tintin, Captain Hadock and Professor Calculus.

The Strand magazine has not been in print for many years, but I am grateful to its superb band of illustrators for producing the immortal pictures of Sherlock Holmes.

A really big thank you to my agent extraordinaire Isabel Atherton at Creative Authors, who set the ball rolling and has been supportive throughout all of the processes of this book.

And finally, thanks to my wife Rachel and my children Kate, Ruth and Andrew for putting up with all those home experiments over the years. And to Lyla, my granddaughter, who had almost as much fun as I did when we made all those bath bombs.

Keith Souter

DISCLAIMER

Although the author and publisher have made every effort to ensure that the information in this book is correct at press time, the author and publisher do not assume and hereby disclaim any liability to any party for any loss, damage, or disruption caused by errors or omissions, whether such errors or omissions result from negligence, accident, or any other cause.

For Sir Patrick Moore,
our national treasure and the greatest
popularizer of science that Britain has ever produced.

Do you remember 'starting science'? I was aged seven, and the whole world opened up to me. Keith Souter takes us back to those heady days, but his book does more than that – it also helps us to understand just how we began, making it easier for us to help and encourage those who are preparing to follow us. Read it, learn from it, and above all enjoy it.

Sir Patrick Moore, writer, researcher, broadcaster and presenter of *The Sky at Night*

The study of natural science begins and ends with observation and experiment, and this rich amalgam of physics, chemistry and biology experiments, which can be done easily at home, is a really fun way to begin.

Peter Duffett-Smith, Reader in Experimental Radio Physics, the Cavendish Laboratory, Cambridge

It's good to remember that science is about finding out how things work, and 'things' and 'work' can range from how to make a battery with blotting paper and salt and vinegar all the way to how to envisage a 'theory of everything' that endeavours to make sense of it all. If the spirit demonstrated by Keith Souter becomes contagious and spreads in the world, there will be more scientists around and less scepticism about science – a most useful and important development!

Professor Ervin Laszlo, philosopher of science, systems theorist, integral theorist, concert pianist and founder president of the Club of Budapest

Eureka! [I have found it!]

Give me a lever long enough and a fulcrum on which to place it, and I shall move the world.

Archimedes (287–212BC), philosopher, mathematician, scientist

Experimental science is the queen of sciences and the goal of all speculation.

Roger Bacon (1214–1294), philosopher and friar

The men of experiment are like the ant, they only collect and use; the reasoners resemble spiders, who make cobwebs out of their own substance. But the bee (the scientist) takes the middle course: it gathers its material from the flowers of the garden and field, but transforms and digests it by a power of its own.

Sir Francis Bacon (1561–1626), philosopher, statesman, scientist

INTRODUCTION

When I was really young I was obsessed with rockets and outer space. I remember when the Soviet Union launched Sputnik 1 and how I watched the sky for what seemed like hours on end in the hope of seeing the first satellite zoom by. Some time later I saw *The Sky at Night* on television, presented by Patrick Moore, a wonderfully charismatic man who seemed to know all about space, the stars and the most distant worlds. I was hooked on science from then on.

It was in a spirit of great expectation and enthusiasm that I approached

Sherlock Holmes's chemistry bench

" HOLMES WAS WORKING HARD OVER A CHEMICAL INVESTIGATION."

my first proper science lesson at school. Unfortunately, my science teacher was not as cool as the subject he claimed to be an expert in. When it became obvious to me that he had no intention of showing me how to make stink bombs I realized that I would have to become an experimenter myself.

The trouble was that I needed to have a proper laboratory. I had been brought up watching *The Munsters* on TV and so wanted to live in a house with a dungeon that had been converted into a lab. A place where retorts could merrily bubble away, gushing out foam and coloured smoke, where machines and gadgets knocked up in an afternoon would whirr, bang and solve the mysteries of science before imploding back into a heap of coils and springs. But we had no dungeon, only a cupboard under the stairs, and that was used to keep mouldy sports equipment and an Ali Baba clothes basket full of dirty washing. So that was no use.

My other great influence in those distant days was the great detective Sherlock Holmes. He shared rooms at 221B Baker Street with Dr John Watson. He had no laboratory, but he did have a chemistry corner. Poor Dr Watson was forever coming home and having to fight his way through fumes in order to save Holmes from poisoning himself with some noxious gas or other. So a science bench was a possibility.

Unfortunately, my parents didn't think so. My experiments with an early chemistry set had left the kitchen table scorched and stained, so the chemistry set mysteriously disappeared. Yet that did not curb my enthusiasm. I was determined to carry on my experiments. I devoured books on popular science, electronics and conjuring. I dreamed of making some incredible discovery that would propel me into an alternate universe, give me super powers, or perhaps something simple like a cure for the common cold.

I was forever trying to repeat school science experiments using everyday things found in the home. My laboratory was the house itself, virtually every room. Although I didn't make any earth-shattering discoveries or travel through time, my impromptu experimentations did help me to learn about science. That interest propelled me to university, to the various science laboratories and the dissecting rooms where I needed to study in order to become a doctor.

And now in this book I want to take you on a journey through the wonderful world of science. Don't be fooled by the title: although it says *Schoolboy Science Remembered*, that is simply because I went to a boys' school myself and it is about my recollections. It could equally have been *Schoolgirl Science Remembered*, except that I was never a girl.

Finally, this is no textbook of science, but rather a pot-pourri of experiments, historical snippets and a few odd facts, all interspersed with the odd conjuring trick. It won't help you to pass any science exams, but it should be fun. In a way this is a trip down memory lane for me, since I will be dredging up those old experiments that I did with things that I found about the house, or which I bought with my meagre pocket money. The dads and even granddads out there will possibly recall many of these experiments and may remember trying them themselves. Anyway, it is my fervent hope to show you how to recreate some of those great old experiments of our schooldays and persuade you that science really *is* cool.

Keith Souter

CHAPTER ONE

THE KITCHEN LABORATORY

The kitchen is, of course, the main laboratory in a house. Laboratory means 'the science work room'. It comes from the Latin *laboratorium*, itself derived from *laborare*, meaning 'to work'.

It amazed me how my mother could take all sorts of raw materials, mix them up, bubble them away in a variety of pans and skillets and transform them into good, tasty meals. Clearly, cooking involved some pretty amazing chemistry.

The electricity and gas that powered this process, the heat, the steam and the energy needed to bring about these wonderful changes, all depended upon physics.

And then what happened when we ate the stuff? Well, we don't need to go too far into that just now (although we will later, when we hit the bath-

The kitchen laboratory has many uses

4

room and visit the loo for an experiment or two!). Suffice it to say that those questions took me off into the wonders of biology.

Effectively, this all made me realize that the kitchen laboratory was the place where the three main sciences of chemistry, physics and biology came together. So let's have a little look.

BUT FIRST: A WORD OF WARNING

It is a fundamental principle of science – and of the kitchen – to take care. Although we are not going to be doing anything dangerous in this book, you should take care with hot liquids, heat and electricity. If you were working in a laboratory at school, you would nowadays be advised to wear goggles when doing experiments involving chemicals. That is some-thing you could consider – I say no more!

A SPOT OF PHYSICS

The ancient Greeks seemed to start it all off. Although there is evidence that the ancient Babylonians performed experiments in optics, mechanics and geometry, it seems that the Greeks were the first people to try and break away from a divine explanation of the universe. Leucippus of Abdera was the first to teach that every event had a natural cause, in the fifth century BC. And with him and other great thinkers, who we shall meet in the pages of this book, the rudiments of science were set down. They called this natural philosophy.

We will come back to him, his pupil Democritus and contemporaries like Empedocles in the following chapters, for they gave us a first sight of an atomic theory. For now, we shall just accept that physics is the science concerned with the study of matter and energy and the way that they interact with each other. Energy can take the form of motion, light, electricity, radiation, gravity and so on. And physics deals with everything from the tiniest subatomic particle to the most distant galaxy. More than that, in the realms of theoretical physics, the field that Albert Einstein was so influential in, a search goes on to find what is called the 'Theory of Everything'.

This is really heady stuff and we shall come back to it at the end of the book. It may be that you will be the one to discover that elusive Theory of Everything one day. If so, you might want to take a hyper-jump to the last chapter to bone up on relativity and quantum mechanics. But if you just want to take one step at a time and have a little fun, then let's stay in the kitchen for a while longer and look at a little kitchen physics.

THE STATES OF MATTER

Kitchens are interesting places where incredible transformations take place. Cooking, baking, roasting, toasting … you name it, it all goes on in the kitchen. It can be a hot, steamy atmosphere. And yet in the fridge, where the temperature drops, food and drinks are kept cool and in the freezer things are frozen so that they remain wholesome for great periods of time.

Water is constantly being used. It is used to cook things in and it is a main constituent of so many of our foods. As I am sure you are well aware, about 70 per cent of the human body itself is made up of water. All life depends upon it.

Water is also a good way to start looking at matter, because ice, water and steam are all present in the kitchen laboratory. These represent the states of matter, which is a good place to start our consideration of physics.

Most substances can exist in different states of matter. This essentially refers to how much heat is contained within the molecules that make up its substance. The more heat is present, the more the molecules move, and so the harder it is to keep them together. So, the state of matter of a substance is dependent upon two things – the temperature and the pressure it is under.

There are three common states of matter for most substances: solid, liquid and gas. Whenever we consider water, we refer to these states as ice, water and steam, or water vapour.

THE FOURTH AND FIFTH STATES OF MATTER

There are, in fact, two more states of matter, which you might not expect to see in the kitchen laboratory. The fourth is **plasma** and the fifth is **superfluid**.

A **plasma** (not to be confused with blood plasma) is an ionized gas bursting with energy, so that the electrons have been released from their atoms and molecules. Thus it is a cloud of protons, neutrons and electrons. You may not believe it, but plasma makes up **99 per cent of the universe**: it is the most abundant state of matter. This is the state that exists inside stars that are undergoing nuclear fusion. You may have heard of 'ball lightning', which is an example of plasma that might manifest on earth.

Superfluids are the opposite of plasmas. They exist only for certain types of molecules when they are cooled to temperatures near absolute zero when it is postulated that things barely move. The atoms collapse into a single quantum, a **Bose–Einstein condensate**. In 1999 scientists at Harvard University in the USA shone light into a Bose–Einstein condensate and found that it slowed the speed of light down to a mere 38 miles an hour. Spooky!

A typical phase equilibrium diagram

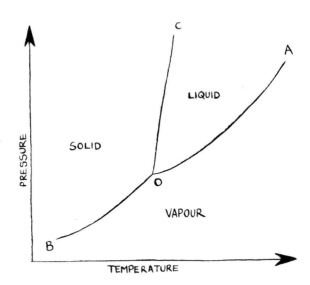

Figure 3 shows a typical **phase equilibrium diagram** for a substance. This relates the phase that the substance will be in at a particular pressure and temperature. It is worth studying this for a few moments, because it will make things clear.

The diagram is divided into three areas corresponding to solid, liquid and gas. Therefore, you can see what conditions of pressure and temperature are needed for any single phase or state of matter for that substance. The lines tell you the conditions of pressure and temperature needed to see two phases at the same time. For example, line OA would give you the pressure and corresponding temperature at which liquid and gas would coexist. The Point O is called the **triple point**. It is the exact condition of pressure and temperature at which all three phases can co-exist. So, any slight shift in the conditions will cause one phase to disappear. And so you can make predictions about the states of matter of that substance. Beyond point A liquid and gas are indistinguishable.

The phase equilibrium diagram for water is a rather special case. You will see that the line OC leans slightly to the left for water, whereas for most other substances it leans to the right. This is because the melting point of ice is lowered when the pressure is raised.

This unusual behaviour of water is related by **Le Chatelier's principle** to the way that it expands or gets bigger when it freezes, whereas most other substances get smaller. By contrast, metals tend to expand as they get hotter.

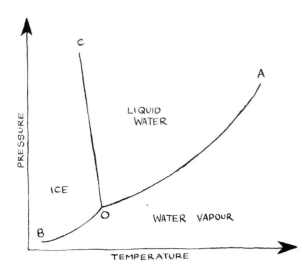

The phase equilibrium diagram for water

LE CHATELIER'S PRINCIPLE

Henry Louis Le Chatelier (1850–1936) is famous for devising the principle of chemical equilibrium. This states that if a chemical system at equilibrium experiences a change in concentration, temperature or total pressure, the equilibrium will shift in order to minimize that change.

At normal atmospheric pressure[1] the freezing point[2] of pure water is 0°C and the boiling point is 100°C. These both change if something is dissolved in the water. The freezing point drops and the boiling point increases. This phenomenon can be very useful in physical chemistry.

Ice

Ice is the solid form of water. In a solid all of the molecules are compressed into a definite shape and volume. They tend to form bonds that hold them into a firm shape.

If you add salt to ice you will drop the freezing point, so that it will turn back to water. This happens when we throw salt on icy roads. The freezing point drops so that the road becomes wet rather than slippy and icy. And you can demonstrate it with your first little experiment, which you can do as a trick next time you are at the dinner table with a glass with ice in front of you.

The Ice-Sewing Experiment
Show how you can sew an ice cube on to a piece of thread or string.

REQUIREMENTS

✓ a glass of water with ice cubes
✓ a piece of thread or string
✓ a salt cellar

METHOD

Challenge the other diners to lift an ice cube using only the thread or string. When they fail, you simply lay the thread across the top of the glass, so that a loop touches an ice cube. Pour salt over the thread and cube. Wait a moment then lift, and behold, the ice cube will be sewn to the thread.

EXPLANATION

The salt lowers the freezing point, so that some ice melts. It freezes over the thread and so the ice cube is sewn!

Ice skating is an example of **regelation.** This is the phenomenon in which an intense pressure will temporarily lower the freezing point of water, so that the skater moves along on a slurry of water. It freezes over immediately to become ice the moment the skate has moved on. The point is that you don't skate on ice at all, you skate on water.

'Sewing' an ice cube

The Ice-Sawing Experiment
See how a heavily weighted wire will saw itself through a block of ice.

REQUIREMENTS
- ✓ a large block of ice (about three inches wide by one inch deep and six inches long)
- ✓ a piece of thin picture hanging wire
- ✓ various weights
- ✓ a supporting beam

METHOD
Support and secure the block of ice on a beam or plank. Tie the weights to either end of the picture frame wire and hang this over the ice block.

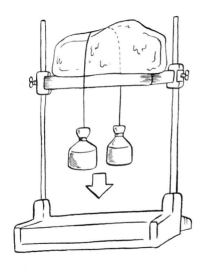

The idea is to attempt this with several paired weights until you see what weights are needed to produce an effect. You should find that the heavier the weight the faster the result. And that result should be that the wire gradually passes through the ice block, but without leaving a cut.

EXPLANATION

Regelation will take place so that the pressure will change ice to water, which allows the weight to sink, causing further ice to change into water. As that happens the water through which the wire has passed will freeze over.

Regelation

Water

Everyone is familiar with water, the essential of life. It is a great example of the liquid phase in which atoms and molecules are in contact with one another and can move over each other, yet cannot escape. They will take on the shape of the container they are in.

We are going to be looking at water in greater depth later in the book and will do several experiments on it and other liquids, so let us now just have a look at water vapour and steam.

Steam

To be correct, steam and water vapour are not quite the same. By steam we really mean only water in its gaseous state above the boiling point. Water vapour is water in the gaseous state plus other gases, like those in air, below the boiling point. Thus you can have water vapour at any temperature from 0° to 100° C.

In this gaseous phase the atoms and molecules are not contained and will tend to disperse.

One thing you may not know is that steam is invisible. It is only when it hits cooler air about it that it forms the clouds of what we think is steam. Next time you boil a kettle look at the spout as the water boils. You will see that there is nothing for about an inch from the spout, and then the steam seems to start.

Now, if you look at the phase diagram again, you will see that as the pressure increases, so the temperature at which water boils will increase. We utilize this in pressure cookers. Here the pressure may be doubled, causing the water and its contents to boil at a higher temperature, thence cooking the food faster. Most modern pressure cookers are designed so that the water within them will boil at a temperature of 110°C to 130°C. At 130°C chemical food reactions take place at three times the rate that they do at normal boiling point.

By contrast, if you go up a mountain the boiling point of water will drop, as the pressure decreases. The problem in cooking food at high altitudes, of course, is that because the water boils at a lower temperature, many of the chemical reactions that depend on reaching a certain temperature will not take place and the food may not be as well cooked.

THE PRESSURE COOKER

This very useful gadget was invented in 1681 by Denis Papin, a French-born British scientist and mathematician. He called it a 'steam digester', because he was investigating a means for extracting the stock from bones. It is essentially a hermetically sealed pot, which allows the steam produced to create an increase in pressure and the temperature will rise. It has been referred to as an anti-mountain for this reason. You will understand why it can be a useful way of cooking at high altitudes.

Papin also did important work on the diving bell and produced the first piston steam engine. The latter was not terribly efficient, yet his contribution led to the development of the steam engine.

Steam power

The first use of steam to power a machine was devised by the Greek mathematician and philosopher Hero of Alexandria in the first century AD. He described the machine, which he called an *aeolipile*, named after Aeolus, the Greek god of the wind, in a book called *Pneumatica*. History simply calls it the Hero engine. Essentially it consisted of a metal sphere, which had two bent spouts at opposite poles of the sphere. The spouts were arranged to point in opposite directions. These worked to jet-propel the sphere round and round on its axis. Effectively, it was the first steam turbine. It is unknown what use he put it to, but it is thought to have been a spectacular feature of a temple.

AN HEROIC EXPERIMENTER

Hero of Alexandria (cAD10–70) was an incredibly able mathematician, philosopher and inventor. Among his other achievements he invented a windwheel, a wind-powered organ, a hydraulic fountain, a thunderclap machine for use in the theatre and the world's first coin-operated vending machine. This latter was used to dispense a set amount of holy water for pilgrims visiting the temple.

The Hero engine is regarded as the world's first steam turbine

In 1698 an English engineer called Thomas Savery built a steam pump designed to pump water out of flooded mines. This was improved upon by Thomas Newcomen in 1712. In 1782 the Scottish engineer James Watt invented the first rotary steam engine that effectively supplanted wind and water power to drive machinery. In 1829 George Stephenson built his Rocket, the first effective locomotive. The world of steam was on its way.

Now it is time for some more experiments.

The Cloud In A Bottle Experiment
You may have heard of a storm in a teacup, but how about a cloud in a bottle?

REQUIREMENTS
✓ a large 2-litre clear plastic drink bottle
✓ tap water
✓ matches

METHOD
Rinse out your bottle and leave a little water in it, just enough to cover the dimples at the bottom. Light a match and let it burn enough to get a good flame. Then blow it out so that it starts smoking. Hold the smoking match inside the bottle so that it fills up with smoke. Then drop it in the bottle and screw on the top. Jostle the bottle to that the match head doesn't melt the plastic. Wait a few moments and the smoke will seem to disappear.

Now just squeeze the bottle hard three or four times and then release. Now wait a few more seconds then squeeze it again and then release. Watch and you will see a cloud start to appear in the bottle.

EXPLANATION
You have actually produced a cloud of smog here! As you increase the pressure you force all of the particles together, the water vapour and the smoke particles are forced more together. Then you release the pressure and you will create a drop in temperature. This cooling will allow condensation of the water valour around the smoke particles as droplets – and a cloud is formed!

And after you have washed your bottle out and cleaned up, you might like to hang on to it for another experiment. This is related to what we have been considering, since it is still about pressure and its effect on gases.

(At this point I would just like to say that I think these plastic bottles are incredibly versatile and permit of many experiments that were far harder to do when I was a lad. We used to have to use glass bottle and bungs! But such is the way that science progresses.)

The Bottled Deep-Sea Diver Experiment

Show how you can make a bottled 'deep-sea' diver go just where you want him.

REQUIREMENTS

✓ a large 2-litre clear plastic drink bottle
✓ tap water
✓ a medicine dropper or a ketchup sachet

METHOD

Fill the bottle to the top with tap water. Take the medicine dropper and compress the bulb to make it suck up water so that it is about quarter full of water. Then place it in the bottle. It should just float under the surface. You may need to adjust the amount of water you have in it to start.

If you are using a ketchup sachet, you may have to do a bit of experimenting to find the right one. It mustn't be too heavy so that it sinks or too light that it protrudes from the surface.

Top up the bottle so that it is completely full and then screw on the top. Now gently squeeze – and if you are doing it as a magic trick, practise squeezing so that it is not obvious that you are doing so. You will find that the 'diver' starts to sink right to the bottom. You can vary the speed he goes by varying the pressure on the sides of the bottle. And when you release the pressure he will come back up again. You can make him go all the way up or sink at will, so that he seems completely under your control.

Make the diver go up or down at your command

EXPLANATION

This is a classical experiment on buoyancy. The diver is called a **Cartesian diver** after the famed French philosopher, mathematician and scientist René Descartes, who did early work on this and many other areas of interest.

When you squeeze you compress the air in the dropper and make more water flow into the tube. This makes it heavier than the surrounding water and it will sink. When you release, the air bubble enlarges and water is forced out so that it gets lighter and rises. It beautifully illustrates the principle of buoyancy.

The buoyancy of an object relates to its ability to float. Thus objects that float are positively buoyant and those that sink are negatively buoyant. If the weight of water that an object displaces is greater than the actual weight of the object, then it will float. If it is less, then it will sink. (And when we come to talk about Archimedes, you will see that this should be a true Eureka moment!)

This principle is how a submarine works. By pumping water in and out of its tanks it can rise or sink. Bony fish (not sharks and the like, which are cartilaginous fish) use this principle in nature. They have a 'swim bladder', which contains air bubbles. They can squeeze or relax it to alter their buoyancy so that they rise, sink or hover at will.

Cartesian diver

AN ORIGINAL THINKER

The French philosopher René Descartes (1596–1650) is considered by many to be the father of modern philosophy and of a particular way of thought. He was the first scientist–philosopher to organize the process of thought and link it to the meaning of one's very existence. This is embodied in his famous argument *cogito ergo sum*: I think, therefore I am.

He is famous for developing the concept known as **Cartesian dualism**: the view that mind and body are separate, distinct substances. He believed that the tools of science and mathematics could be used to explain and predict events in the physical world. Reductionism, the belief that complex things can be reduced to simpler, more fundamental things analysis of things, was a natural result.

CHAPTER TWO

COOKING CHEMISTRY

Now let us leave physics for a while and look at some of the chemical re-actions that go on in the kitchen laboratory. Later on we will be doing some good old-fashioned fizzy experiments, but right now I want to focus on some of the things that happen when you prepare food. It is all useful stuff, believe me, especially if you have aspirations to become a celebrity chef and want to make oodles of dough (or should that be a celebrity baker?).

Never mind. We shall be looking at the principles of baking too.

IT STARTED WITH A PRANG

When I was at school all of the teachers seemed old. Many of them had fought in the Second World War and were definitely oldish, but we had a couple who seemed positively ancient and who may have fought in the Great War. One was a mathematics teacher, who must have known Pythagoras himself, and the other was my chemistry master, known to all and sundry as 'Prang'.

I have to describe this fascinating chap. He was a big man with a handlebar moustache, thick, horn-rimmed glasses and a curly pipe that no one ever saw him light. He walked with a slight limp. It was widely rumoured that this was a result of an injury he sustained during the War, when he 'pranged' his Sopwith Camel somewhere over the Western Front.

While all of the other teachers had cars, Prang rode an ancient motor-bike dressed in a great coat, gauntlets and goggles. He certainly looked as though he could have been a chum of Biggles, the famous fictional Great War flying ace.

Anyway, that was reckoned to be the reason for his nickname. Whether there was any truth in it or not, Prang would neither confirm nor refute. He just grinned whenever anyone asked him and twirled the ends of his great moustache.

Back in those days science teachers didn't wear lab coats. Prang certainly did not. He wore a black teacher's gown over a tweed suit. The elbows of his jacket had leather pads sewn on and the sleeves had the odd hole from

There were many rumours as to why he was nicknamed 'Prang'

some acid burn or other. These were the days before health and safety had ever been heard of and so experiments were a lot more fun.

They were not always easy, though. Prang would saunter about the lab looking at our efforts at whatever experiment he was teaching us about. I can still hear his oft-repeated instructions: 'Precision, boys! You need the exact quantities and the exact conditions, get those right and then – bingo! The reaction will work according to the formula. If not, then it isn't chemistry, it is just cookery!'

I remember recounting this at home, much to my mother's disdain. 'That's all very well,' she said in an aggrieved voice. 'And what does he eat in his house? Litmus paper and chemicals? Tell him that cooking is proper science, never mind his chemistry.'

I didn't argue with her.

Nor did I tell Prang what she said. I did, however, note similarities between chemistry and cooking. Just as my mum didn't always get the recipe right, so too did Prang occasionally botch an experiment and either fill the fume cupboard with an unexpectedly noxious gas, or blow up some piece of apparatus, leaving a chemical concoction of entirely the wrong colour to flow over the bench.

Ever since then I have called such cooking disasters or botched experiments 'Prangs'. And, I should add, I do so with the greatest of respect, since Prang was the catalyst that fired my passion for science.

YOU NEED TO EXPERIMENT!

I had not been in Prang's chemistry class for long before I asked him how you make stink bombs. He looked at me in a pitying way that made me squirm.

'You come to my class and instead of wanting to know about the wonders of chemistry you want to know how to make some sort of stupid joke? A stink bomb?'

I gulped and nodded.

'And do you think the headmaster would take kindly to me using the school's chemistry laboratory for such a banal instruction?'

I sort of gurgled and squirmed a bit more.

'You need to use your brain, boy. You need to experiment yourself. That is how you do science – formulate a question, work out a suitable experiment, then put it to the test. Then you look at your results and make a suitable conclusion.'

'You mean I should try to make a stink bomb myself, Sir?' I asked.

Again, the pitying stare, then with a sigh he said: 'When you are ready. When you have enough knowledge. When you have learned a bit more science and you understand what makes a good experiment. For now I want you to just observe and think.'

He produced his pipe and tapped his teeth with the stem.

'Do you like cocoa?'

'I have it every night, Sir. My mum makes it for us.'

'Does she always do it exactly right?'

I wondered what he meant. I supposed he was talking about getting the quantities of the ingredients right. 'Well Sir, sometimes it tastes funny. Sometimes she lets the milk boil over.'

'Ah, then there you have the makings of an experiment. Be an observer and use the senses you were born with.'

And that was that. He wouldn't say any more. I had to go away and *think*.

The cocoa experiment – part 1

Well, even though I racked my brains, I couldn't think what he was going on about. Perhaps Prang was going a bit loopy, I wondered. He said that I had to experiment, but that I should be an observer and use my senses. But which senses – taste, sight, hearing, smell?

Then it struck me. The experiment was just to watch my mum make the cocoa. He obviously meant that I should watch her make it, I should taste it and I should smell it.

I didn't see how that would help me to make a stink bomb, but I gave it a go. I watched her do it for a week. I drank and smelled my cocoa each time and concluded that it tasted a bit different each time. I wasn't sure, but perhaps it also smelled a bit different.

The whole experiment seemed to have been a waste of time, not even a proper Prang. It occurred to me that he was just making the point that cooking and cocoa making were not precise, unlike his precious chemistry. So I had more or less lost interest in cocoa until one night mum was listening to the radio as she boiled the milk. I was reading a comic at the table and there was this sudden hissing noise. We both turned to see the milk foaming out of the pan on to the hot hob where it produced copious amounts of smoke.

As my mum set about cleaning it all up, I wrinkled my nose and gagged. The kitchen smelled awful.

'That's the trouble with boiling milk,' she explained. 'You have to watch it like a hawk. It boils over in an instant.'

'Eureka!' I cried. 'Rotten eggs! Burned milk smells like rotten eggs!'

I didn't know why then, and if you want to know, then go straight to the next chapter on Milk, Butter and Cheese to find out. But there is an additional point to this little anecdote, because it shows that science is often like that. Experiments can be boring, they may take a long time, and then, when you are not quite ready for it, the unexpected happens. Some of our greatest scientific discoveries have come about that way.

Prang taught me that.

FAMOUS PRANGS THAT TURNED INTO EUREKAS

Some of the greatest discoveries have been chance observations of unrelated phenomena that triggered an idea, or they have been unexpected side effects or results encountered during another experiments.

Penicillin In 1928 Sir Alexander Fleming was investigating Staphylococcal cultures in Petri dishes when he discovered that fungal contamination of the dishes with fungal colonies resulted in inhibition of growth of the Staphylococcal colonies. Further research revealed that something in the fungus, which was from a Penicillium species, actually killed the Staphylococci. After some months he called it Penicillin. It took several years before the antibiotic Penicillin could be usefully prescribed. In 1945, Fleming received the Nobel Prize for Medicine together Howard Walter Florey and Ernst Boris Chain, who developed the medicine.

Microwave oven   In the 1940s Percy Spencer, a self-taught engineer, was working for a company building magnetrons for radar equipment. While working with an active machine he noticed that a peanut chocolate bar in his pocket had melted. Realizing that microwaves from the machine must have been responsible he experimented and found that the microwaves could cook food. The first food he cooked was popcorn (which we shall look at in Chapter Nine on Floppy Vegetables and Crispy Fruit). The second was an egg, which exploded. In 1945 his company took out a patent for the microwave cooking process and in 1947 the first microwave oven was produced.

Saccharin   In 1879 Constantin Fahlberg was working on coal tar derivatives in a chemistry laboratory at the Johns Hopkins University in America. He spilled a substance on his hand and licked it, finding to his surprise that it was incredibly sweet. He patented his discovery and the most famous sweetener in the world made him a rich man. His boss, Ira Remsen, is also credited with the discovery, but failed to gain any money from it.

X-rays   In 1895 William Conrad Röntgen, a German physicist, discovered a curious sort of ray while experimenting with a cathode ray tube. This ray was capable of passing through various objects and through human tissue, but was unable to pass through lead. Soon after, he took a photograph of his wife's hand, which clearly showed the skeletal structure. Not knowing what to call this ray, he used the term X-ray, by which it is known today. It transformed medicine and among many awards he was given the first Nobel Prize for Physics in 1901.

THE STAFF OF LIFE

We are going to start with bread. You might not think it, but bread making is a fantastic amalgam of biology and chemistry. It is worth the effort of making your own bread and understanding the processes that are involved.

But first, a little bit of history never did anyone any harm. Bread is called the staff of life because it is regarded as a staple food. That means it is basic food within a society's diet, which can be kept or readily produced throughout the year.

Many cultures throughout the world make bread. Who was the first is unknown, but the ancient Egyptians left written records about the making of bread, and tomb paintings from as far back as 4,000BC actually show bread being made.

The Greeks and the Romans were great bread-makers. Indeed, when Mount Vesuvius erupted in AD79 people were busily going about their daily lives. The lava flow and volcanic ash that engulfed them effectively froze that tragic day in time. Archaeologists have excavated bakers' ovens containing loaves that had been baking on the day.

Essentially, bread is made by baking a dough made from water, a little salt and some form of ground cereal. Which one is used really depends upon which type of cereal is easiest grown in a particular country. This tends to be a reflection of the climate of the country. In most of western Europe we use wheat, but in Finland they use barley. In Ethiopia the high-protein grain called *teff* is used to produce a type of sour, spongy bread called *injera*.

Bread can be either leavened or unleavened. Leavened means that some agent has been added to the dough in order to make it rise. Unleavened bread has no such help and so unrisen bread is produced. Examples of unleavened bread are *matzows*, *chappatis*, *naans* and *tortillas*.

Leavened bread is the type we are most familiar with in the western diet. It is made by using a leavening agent to make the dough rise. The two main leavening agents in use are baking powder or yeast. Let's look at yeast, and then it is time for a quick experiment.

Yeasts all around you

That's right – there are yeasts all about. Yeasts belong to the fungus kingdom, along with toadstools, mushrooms and moulds. There are about

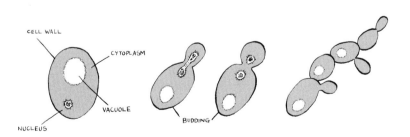

Yeast budding

1,500 known species of yeast. *Saccharomyces cerevisiae* is the type that is used in baking bread and brewing beer and wine-making. For this reason it is commonly known as Brewer's Yeast. This consists of single-celled organisms that grow by a curious type of cell division called 'budding'. They can then grow into microscopic threads that soon fragment into individual cells again.

One gram of yeast will hold about 25 billion cells!

Humankind has always been interested in this particular yeast because of its ability to make bread rise, but also because it can produce alcohol. It does this in two separate ways, both of which involve metabolizing glucose in order to produce energy. It can do it either **aerobically**, meaning with oxygen during the process of respiration, or **anaerobically**, without oxygen during the process of fermentation.

1) **Respiration – aerobic**
   Glucose + oxygen $\rightarrow$ water + carbon dioxide + energy
   $C_6H_{12}O_6 + 6O_2 \rightarrow 6H_2O + 6CO_2 + 674$ calories of energy

2) **Fermentation – anaerobic**
   Glucose $\rightarrow$ carbon dioxide + ethyl alcohol + energy
   $C_6H_{12}O_6 \rightarrow 2CO_2 + 2C_2H_5OH + 22$ calories of energy

The energy that is generated is used to fuel chemical reactions within the yeast cells and to promote growth of the yeast culture. Thus the yeast cells will rapidly multiply as they produce carbon dioxide. Note that the energy it produces is much greater when the yeast is allowed to respire rather than ferment. If yeast is given a choice of reactions it will 'prefer' to respire.

Now, the first reaction is of most use in baking bread, but the second is most valuable in making alcohol. Both of these reactions will actually take place in both brewing and baking, but different strains of *Saccharomyces cerevisiae* have been produced so that the baking type will produce carbon dioxide more rapidly.

In brewing, you strive to create anaerobic conditions by restricting oxygen. Thus the yeast will ferment the sugar. It will then tend to turn up to 15 per cent of the liquid volume into alcohol. Wine makers will stop fermentation before this point, so that they make a wine of about 11 to 12 per cent alcohol.

In baking, the yeast has access to oxygen so it will reproduce rapidly and will produce carbon dioxide rapidly. When this is added to the dough, it will form bubbles in the dough, causing it to rise. When you bake the bread the alcohol that is formed in the dough will be burned away. There will be some alcohol, since both reactions will take place, although the main one will be respiration. And this is just as well, or you could get drunk every time you have toast.

Time for that experiment …

The Leavening Agent Experiment
Can you use yeast or baking powder to blow up a balloon?

REQUIREMENTS
✓ 2 milk bottles
✓ 1 sachet of dried yeast or ½ an ounce of fresh yeast. (Dried yeast comes in the form of tiny spheres of yeast. When soaked in water they reconstitute and get ready to attack sugars. Fresh yeast is usually available from your baker or the bread counter of a supermarket. It comes as a soft putty-coloured block.)
✓ 2 tablespoons of sugar
✓ 1 tablespoon of baking powder
✓ 2 cups of warm water, 1 for each bottle. This should be 'hand-hot' or bearable to the touch. If it is too hot you kill the yeast.
✓ 2 balloons

METHOD
Firstly, prepare the yeast. Put the yeast and the sugar into a jug. Mix the yeast and the sugar together. If using the fresh yeast you need to keep mixing it until it forms a paste. This will very quickly form into a thick liquid. Next add the water and stir it all together. Now pour this into the bottle. Finally, stretch the balloon over the bottle top. Now just add the baking powder to the other cup of water and stir. Then put it in the other bottle (it does not need sugar) and put the other balloon over the top. You will find that both balloons gradually fill up. And probably the baking powder will have gone up like *a balloon*!

EXPLANATION
Oh come on, you know what has happened! At least with the yeast. But what about the baking powder?

Well, baking powder is a mix of sodium bicarbonate, some form of starch (usually cornstarch) and a weak acid (usually tartaric acid). When the powder is added to water the chemicals dissolve and immediately effervesce as carbon dioxide is given off. Thus:

$$NaHCo3 \; + \; H^+ \; \rightarrow \; Na^+ \; + \; CO_2 \; + \; H_2O$$

CAKE CHEMISTRY AND CHEMICAL LEAVENING AGENTS

These cause a lot of confusion to people. As mentioned earlier, baking powder is a mixture of sodium bicarbonate and a weak acid and starch. Baking soda is just another name for sodium bicarbonate. Both baking powder and baking soda are leavening agents. Confusion occurs about the names and the constituents, and also in recipes, when both are used at the same time.

Either agent will cause a release of carbon dioxide, which is what is wanted. They are used in recipes that have batter, a mixture of flour and liquid and usually eggs. They are mixed so that they produce a liquid in which bubbles of air will have formed as you mix. The leavening agent releases carbon dioxide, which will cause the bubbles to get bigger, as well as adding many more bubbles of just carbon dioxide.

When baking powder is used it works by causing an acid-base reaction. This will have an acidic aftertaste, which is neutralized by adding more baking soda, or sodium bicarbonate, which is an alkali. The starch is added to baking powder in order to absorb the water that is formed in the reaction.

Generally, chemical leavening agents are used in batter mixtures rather than stiff dough. Thus yeast is used for bread and chemical leavening agents are used for cakes, biscuits and scones. The reaction starts in the mixture, but continues as the mixture is baked in the oven. You can repeat the balloon experiment with water at different temperatures to check this out. Add hot water to the coolest mix and see what happens.

So now you will have a good idea about the basic chemistry in baking a cake.

Now that you have a couple of balloons full of carbon dioxide, why don't you test them?

The test for carbon dioxide

In the laboratory at school the test for carbon dioxide is to pass the gas through lime water – calcium hydroxide, $Ca(OH)_2$ – which will then turn a milky colour as calcium carbonate is formed, thus:

$$Ca(OH)_2 + CO_2 = CaCO_3 \downarrow + H_2O$$

Calcium hydroxide + carbon dioxide = calcium carbonate + water

But you can also test it by flowing it over moistened blue litmus paper, which will turn red. Or over universal indicator, which will turn orange, or over a natural indicator, as in the chapter about Things that Fizz. Alternatively, you could just empty the balloon into an empty bottle and gently pour it over a lit candle. It will extinguish the flame. That's probably the easiest way for now. It does so because CO_2 is quite a dense gas, so you can pour it from one glass to another.

USES OF CARBON DIOXIDE

- in fire extinguishers to put out oil based or electrical fires
- in carbonated drinks, e.g. soda water, lemonade
- in baking and the food industry
- in arc welding
- in the plastic industry
- in lasers
- as a coolant
- dry ice, or frozen carbon dioxide, is used theatrically to produce copious amounts of 'smoke'

Right. So what about making that bread?

You Knead To Dough This Experiment

OK, that is a corny pun, but let's try making this loaf. Remember, this is a practical demonstration of physics, chemistry and biology – and you can work that out!

REQUIREMENTS

To make a one-pound loaf:
- ✓ 1 pound of strong white plain flour (Make sure that it is plain. Do *not* use self-raising flour, which is made up of plain flour, salt and baking powder as a leavening agent)
- ✓ 2 teaspoons of salt (or less)
- ✓ 2 teaspoons of sugar
- ✓ 1 ounce (25 grams) of fresh yeast
- ✓ ½ pint of hand-hot water
- ✓ 1 tablespoon of olive oil (optional)

METHOD

In a jug mix the yeast and the sugar with a wooden spoon. As you already know, it will form a paste. Then add half of your water and stir this up. Sprinkle a pinch of flour over the surface of the liquid and then put this somewhere warm to let it rise. It will gradually foam as it ferments.

Meanwhile, put the flour and salt in a large bowl. Add the olive oil and stir it in well. Put this somewhere warm as well.

Once the yeast mix has formed a foam head of about two inches you are ready to add to the flour.

Form a well in the middle of the flour and pour the yeast mix in. Then

The ingredients for the dough experiment

stir it in well. Now gradually add the rest of the water, stirring well all the time. You are aiming to get a consistency that will form into a ball. This needs a bit of experimenting, but you will gradually get it right. If you have added too much water then you can add a little more flour.

What reactions are taking place here?

It kneads some
rough treatment!

Now get your clean hands in. Knead the dough, for that is what it is now. When it is well formed, take it out, and on a lightly floured working surface knead it for about 8–10 minutes. Kneading basically means folding the dough over and over again, each time stretching and pressing it. You will find that it changes texture as you do so and becomes quite elastic.

Then put the dough back in the bowl and cover it with a dampened cloth. Put it somewhere warm again and allow it to rise for about an hour. When you look at it again it will have doubled in size. You then take it out and knead it again back to its original size. Then you work it into a sausage shape and put that on a baking tray that you have greased with a knob of butter. Cover it with the cloth again and put it on a cool surface for a couple of hours. It will rise again. Once it has done so, make about three cuts on the top of the dough (this is so that it does not burst as it rises in the oven).

Preheat the oven to 250°C or 500°F (this will probably be the oven's highest temperature). Using oven gloves put the baking tray with the dough sausage into the oven on the middle rung and leave it there for 25–30 minutes. Just keep an eye on it.

It should turn a beautiful golden colour. When you take it out, turn it

The finished product

upside down (again with oven gloves). It should sound hollow in the middle if you tap it. If it doesn't sound hollow it is not ready.

Well done: you have just baked your loaf!

WHAT HAS HAPPENED?

Quite a lot, actually. Firstly, we need to consider what flour is actually made up of. It contains two types of starch, **amylase** and **amylopectin**, plus a variety of proteins, some of which are soluble in water and others which are insoluble. The insoluble ones are the important ones. There are two types that we need to consider: the **gliadins** and the **glutenins**.

The glutenins are very large molecules and the gliadins are very small, almost a thousandth the size of the glutenins. Both are like long strings that have been balled up. When you knead the dough you unravel those balls and, gradually, hydrogen bonds and sulphur bridges develop between the two types of protein to bind them together. This process is referred to as 'developing the gluten'. You have changed the proteins and developed a new substance.

Gluten[3] makes the dough fluffy and elastic and gives it the right texture so that it will trap the bubbles of carbon dioxide that are formed by the fermentation and the respiration of the yeast. When you look at a slice of your bread you will see that it is full of tiny bubbles.

And that is how you make bread.

But what about that lovely golden brown crust?

Well, that is quite another thing, which we shall consider now.

The Maillard reaction

I was always intrigued that whenever something was cooked it changed colour, like the loaf of bread and like toast. Why is that, do you think? Is it just a case of it being part of a burning process, like scorching paper?

Well, no, it isn't. It is a very specific chemical reaction called the Maillard reaction. It is one of the basic chemical reactions that take place in much of cooking, and it is one of four types of browning reaction. You mum will be impressed that you know all about this.

Browning

The browning of food is both desirable and undesirable. It is desirable in that in some cases it helps the food to taste and look better. It can be undesirable in that it can make food look off, such as when fruits go brown or discoloured or when cut mushrooms go black.

We can divide this browning effect into two broad types: **enzymatic browning** and **non-enzymatic browning**. We will consider **enzymes** in Chapter Six on Fizzics and enzymatic browning in Chapter Nine on Floppy Vegetables and Crispy Fruit.

For now, I am just going to consider the Maillard reaction. This is of great importance because it is responsible for the browning and flavouring of toast, biscuits, coffee, the browning of meat, the grilling of sausages and the browning of beers.

The Maillard reaction was first described by Louis Camille Maillard in 1912, when he was trying to synthesize proteins. What he described is actually a series of chemical reactions that take place between sugars and the amino acids that make up some proteins. When molecules containing an amine group ($-NH_2$), typically an amino acid, meet sugar molecules like glucose in the presence of heat, water molecules are then eliminated, forming a compound called a **Schiff base**. This is rapidly changed into another compound, called an **Amadori product**. This then reacts with other molecules to produce a variety of ring-like or cyclical aromatic molecules. These produce the tantalizing smell and flavour of cooked food.

This is an extremely complex process that may produce two or three hundred of these aromatic chemicals during the cooking process. And that is where the skill of cooking comes in – when one knows how to cook the food to produce the right aromas and flavours.

The Maillard reaction only takes place at high temperatures, however. That is why cooks use fats or oils to baste food or to fry them in. When you do that you attain temperatures well above 100°C. That is what you need to produce a Maillard reaction. If you don't hit that temperature, you will not brown the meat or the food and you will not produce the range of aromatic compounds. That is why boiling food does not brown it. Similarly, the microwave will not produce a Maillard reaction, because it works by causing the water in the food to boil. It will only boil at 100°C, which is too low to induce the Maillard reaction.

Let's raise a toast to Louis Camille Maillard

Hence microwavable food will not be crisp and will not smell as good or turn a beautiful golden brown. It really is one of the most important reactions in cooking chemistry.

And that is what produces that lovely golden brown crust on your loaf.

Toast

People have been making toast for hundreds of years. The method used until the end of the nineteenth century was to use a long fork or trident to spear a slice of bread and hold it in front of an open fire. As you now know, it was held until the Maillard reaction started to take place between the sugars and amino acids in the bread.

In 1893 a British company, Crompton & Co, patented the first electric toaster. Who actually came up with the idea is unknown. It was not a great success, however, and it was not until 1910 that the first effective electric toaster was produced in the USA.

The temperatures in a toaster can be somewhere of the order of 300°C plus. If you leave the toast in too long, then it goes black instead of the golden brown that you want. This is not due to further Maillard reaction. What happens is that you start to carbonize the bread. In other words, you burn the toast. This is supposedly what King Alfred the Great did to some cakes that he was supposed to be looking after. As a reward, the old lady he was staying with boxed his ears. There is a message there somewhere.

USES OF THE MAILLARD REACTION

- cooking
- bread-making
- toasting bread
- roasting coffee
- producing silage!

CHAPTER THREE

MILK, BUTTER, CHEESE

Little Miss Muffet
sat on a tuffet
eating some curds and whey.
Along came a spider
and sat down beside her
and frightened Miss Muffet away.

I am sure that you will be familiar with the old nursery rhyme about Miss Muffett. Like most nursery rhymes, it is a curious little tale. And like many of them, there is in fact a story behind it. I am going to talk about it for a few moments, because it has some relevance to this chapter.

The nursery rhyme was first published in 1805, but is thought to refer to a Dr Thomas Muffet (1553–1604), an English doctor and naturalist. In the 1580s he studied silkworms in Italy and while he was there developed a passion for insects and spiders. He studied and wrote about them. He was also interested in nutrition and health and wrote a book about it, called *Health's Improvement*.

Dr Muffet met many famous and important scientists of his day, including the great Tycho Brahe, whom we shall meet again in Chapter Thirteen on Through the Telescope. Little Miss Muffet is thought to be his step-daughter. It would certainly fit in with Dr Muffet's passion about spiders, and possibly his step-daughter's phobia of them. And of course, the image of her eating her curds and whey could be an image straight out of his book.

The use of whey in medicine was first practised by the ancient Greeks.

Little Miss Muffet

Dr Muffet studied this ancient system and based his practice upon it. Whey was thought to be effective as a tonic, and was widely used to aid digestion, purify the blood, protect against poisoning and prevent liver disorders, obesity and arthritis, and help skin problems.

When milk is left to curdle (or when it is made to curdle) it separates into a thin liquid called whey and a lumpy solid called curds. These are actually very interesting, as we shall now see.

Milk: a natural emulsion

Milk is an emulsion of fat and water. An emulsion is a mixture of two **immiscible** or unblendable liquids that have been mixed together so well that one is dispersed in the other as tiny globules. A protein called **casein** acts as an emulsifying agent to prevent the globules from coalescing, which would result in two distinct layers being formed.

As I am sure you will know, milk in the UK is pasteurized, which is a process that slows down microbial growth. The process was first described by the famous French chemist and microbiologist Louis Pasteur.

Milk also tends to be available as full-cream milk, which contains cream, or as semi-skimmed, which has had about half its fat content skimmed away, or skimmed, which has little fat left. They are all still emulsions. A bottle of full-cream milk will have cream at the top, since it is lighter than the rest of the milk.

The cocoa experiment – part 2

In the last chapter I described the night that my mother let the milk boil over as she was making cocoa. There was an awful smell of rotten eggs. I didn't understand why it should smell as it did, but then I didn't have the advantage of reading this book! To understand it I need to explain just why milk boils over the way that it does.

You will not see it when you look at a pint of milk, but in actual fact the whole of the milk is in continual motion. The tiny globules are buzzing about all the time. This is called Brownian motion. It was first described by the botanist Robert Brown in 1827 (more of him in Chapter Twelve on Down the Microscope). When you heat milk these globules really start moving so that they collide, then coalesce into bigger globules. Then once the temperature reaches about 80°C the casein protein coagulates. Now, as I mentioned above, the casein is the emulsifying agent that keeps the two immiscible or unblendable liquids dispersed. When it coagulates it can no longer do that, so the globules begin to form a continuous layer. You may have heard of people describing this as the skin of the milk. If you watch milk boiling you will see this skin gradually form. Now, water

Burning Milk

vapour starts to form and rises as masses of minute bubbles from the bottom of the pan. These get trapped beneath the skin, so that it rises under the pressure of the constant production of water vapour bubbles. And before your very eyes the milk rises very rapidly, and then boils over.

When the milk boils over the amino acids that make up the milk proteins are broken down by the intense heat of the cooker ring or hob. This causes sulphur atoms to be released. A chemical reaction takes place between them and the hydrogen ions in the milk, thence producing hydrogen sulphide, H_2S, which is the gas that is released in a stink bomb.

Eureka! It smells just like rotten eggs.

Colloids, emulsions and the Tyndall effect

This is a good point at which to clear something up. A **solution** is technically a uniform mixture in which one substance (the **solute**) is dissolved in another substance (the **solvent**). For example, in a salt solution, salt is dissolved in water.

A **colloid** is another type of mixture in which one substance is evenly distributed throughout another without being dissolved in it. The particles of the substance are too big to be dissolved, but small enough to be dispersed. A colloid system can be solid, liquid or gas. An **emulsion** is a special type of colloid in which one of the substances is in a liquid form.

Milk, vinaigrette dressing, mayonnaise, butter and photographic film are all common emulsions. Emulsions are also used in medicine, both externally as skin creams and ointments, and internally as a means of delivering drugs to the body.

If you shine a bright light through a solution you will simply illuminate the solution. On the other hand, if you shine a bright light through a colloid you will get light scattering. Effectively, you will see a distinct path of the beam of light. This happens with car headlights in the fog, when you see a definite beam. And it happens if you shine a beam through smoke. This is called the Tyndall effect, and it is a good test for the presence of a colloid.

Professor John Tyndall (1820–1893) was an English physicist who did important work on magnetism, heat and the atmosphere. He is best known, however, for the Tyndall effect, which occurs when light is shone through a colloid. When the dispersed particles are larger than the wavelength of the light, then you will get light scattering. You will see the beam.

A little experiment is called for to demonstrate.

The Milky Tyndall Effect Experiment

This is a quite fascinating phenomenon, which will, I think, surprise you.

REQUIREMENTS

✓ a test tube or thin glass
✓ very weak milk emulsion
✓ a darkened room
✓ bright narrow-beamed torch (you can improvise by using a piece of cardboard with a hole over the torch light)
✓ a pair of Polaroid spectacles (sunglasses)

METHOD

Put just a few drops of milk in the glass and fill it up with water. You will note that it has a very slight grey–blue tinge. That is significant!

In a darkened room, shine the torch through the glass. You will see a definite beam passing through the liquid. Look closely and it will seem to be slightly blue. Now aim the beam through the glass at a white wall. You will see that the spot of light on the wall has a red tinge. Indeed, if you look through the glass at the light source, it will be shining red.

Finally, if you look at the beam through the polarized spectacles, rotating them slightly until this occurs, you will see the beam darken.

EXPLANATION

You have produced a Tyndall effect. This is all about light scattering. The dispersed globules in this weak emulsion scatter the shorter blue wavelengths of light more strongly than they do the red wavelengths. The beam of light that you see going through the emulsion is caused by the scattered blue rays. The light spot on the wall is unscattered red rays, hence the red tinge.

The blue rays are polarized, which is why the beam appears darker when you look through the polarized sunglasses. It is the same reason that the sky seems a darker blue when you use polarized sunglasses on a sunny day.

THE IMPOSSIBLE MILK BOTTLE AND MILK BOTTLE TOP TRICK

This is a neat little trick that will surprise your family and friends. Get an empty milk bottle and wash the bottle top. Bend the bottle top in half so that it can slip easily into the neck of the bottle. Now lay the bottle on its side and put the bent top in the bottle mouth. Now with it in that position challenge anyone to blow the cap into the bottle. They will not be able to do it! Each time they try the cap will be blown out of the bottle.

EXPLANATION

By blowing on the cap you blow air into the bottle – and this increase in pressure forces the bottle top out!

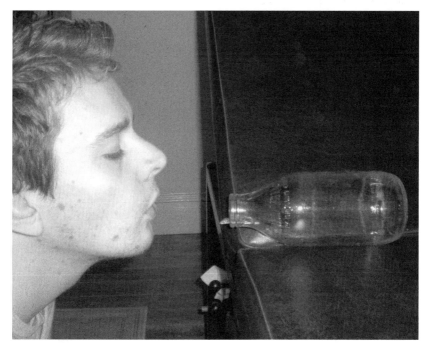

It is impossible!

The Butter Churn Experiment

In the last chapter you learned how to make bread. Now let's see if you can make something to go on it – butter. Ask your parents first, of course.

REQUIREMENTS

- ✓ 500 millilitres or 500 grams of thick whipping cream or double cream
- ✓ a clean coffee jar with a screw-on top
- ✓ a marble, which is clean and hygienic (soak it in boiled water for an hour)
- ✓ a pinch of salt
- ✓ a large bowl and a sieve

METHOD

Chill the whipping cream, the marble and the jar in the fridge for an hour. Pour the cream into the jar and pop in the marble. Screw on the lid and start shaking the jar. You will need a lot of energy, because you are going to do this for up to half an hour. (Perhaps your parents will help.)

You will hear the marble rattling about, but after about 15 minutes you will stop hearing it. The cream will start to get a lot thicker and will stick to the sides. Then after a while you will start to hear the marble again!

Your home-made butter churn

The cream will come off the jar sides and a liquid will appear, in which are lumps of butter. This part of the process may take another quarter of an hour. Then unscrew the lid and pour the liquid and butter into the sieve above the bowl.

You have successfully churned the cream into butter and buttermilk. The buttermilk is a tasty drink in its own right. Now collect the butter in a bowl and pour cold water over it. Pour the water away. Keep doing this until the water stops looking milky and comes away clear. Effectively you are washing any further buttermilk away, since this can make the butter sour.

Add the salt (or not if your parents don't use salted butter) and with a couple of wooden spoons compress the butter against the bowl sides, or between the spoons, again and again until you have squeezed all of the buttermilk away. Traditionally, this is done with a couple of sycamore wood spatulae, called 'Scotch hands'.

EXPLANATION

Very simply, you have transformed a fat in water emulsion into a water in fat emulsion. Butter, like milk, is still an emulsion.

Butter never tasted so good

There are three things that have happened in the process. The churning breaks the membranes of the fat globules, allowing them to coalesce into bigger globules or lumps of fat. These are called butter grains. Further churning traps air in the fat, so that a thick foam is formed. This traps the fluid. Further churning bursts these bubbles and releases the fluid, the buttermilk, and the butter will start to clump.

You have made butter.

EMULSIFIERS AND DEMULSIFIERS

Emulsifiers or **emulsifying agents** help two immiscible or unblendable liquids to form and stabilize an emulsion.

Casein is an emulsifying agent in milk.

When your mum makes a vinaigrette dressing for a salad she mixes vinegar and oil, salt, pepper and a pinch of mustard. The mustard is the emulsifying agent that will turn the vinegar and oil into an emulsion.

When you wash dishes you use washing-up liquid. This is a detergent, which breaks the grease and oil globules up into very small ones. You can then wash the emulsion off, whereas the grease would stay. This technique is used to deal with oil slicks from tanker leaks at sea.

This is also the principle of soap.

Demulsifiers or **emulsion splitting agents** reverse this process and cause an emulsion to split into its two component immiscible liquids.

Acetic acid (vinegar) or citric acid added to milk will split the water and fat components.

Demulsifiers are of great importance in the treatment and processing of crude oil, which may well have been mixed with salt water.

The Cheese Experiment

And, of course, cheese is also a product of milk, so let's experiment with making some curd or cottage cheese.

REQUIREMENTS

✓ 1 pint of lukewarm full-cream milk (ideally heated to about 32°C or 90°F)
✓ 2 bowls
✓ 10 drops of vegetarian rennet
✓ a wooden spoon
✓ a muslin cloth
✓ a sieve
✓ a pinch of salt

METHOD

Heat the milk to about 32°C or 90°F, but no hotter. This is at about the temperature that a really hot bath would be. When it gets to the hot-bath heat, take it off. Now pour the milk into a bowl and add 10 drops of rennet. Give it a good stir then cover with the muslin cloth and set it aside in a warm room for between 24 and 48 hours. The milk will separate into curds and whey.

Now put the muslin in the sieve and strain the curds, so that the whey accumulates in the second bowl. You can dispose of this or you can drink it if you wish. Gather the ends of the muslin and squeeze as much whey out of the curds as you can. Then just leave it in the sieve to drain as much whey as possible overnight. Next day, add a pinch of salt (or not) and mix.

You have made cottage cheese, which you can eat on toast or crackers or as part of a salad.

EXPLANATION

Cottage cheese is thought to be called this because it could easily be made in cottages with left-over milk after butter-making. It is also called curd

Miss Muffet's curds and whey and the vegetarian rennet that did the trick

Cottage cheese

cheese. It has to be eaten fresh, preferably within three or four days of you making it.

The heating to hot-bath temperature will tend to make the casein start to coagulate, as I mentioned in the Cocoa Experiment – part 2. The next phase is done enzymatically. The reason you don't want your milk too hot is because enzymes are inactivated at too high a temperature.

It is traditional to use rennet, which is a natural complex of enzymes derived from the fourth chamber of a calf's stomach. The main enzyme in this complex is called rennin, which has the action of clotting or coagulating milk. That is the basis of the process.

It is likely that back in the dim, distant past people discovered that milk put into a skin made from the stomach of a calf clotted and turned to cheese. People are not keen on this source nowadays, and so vegetarian rennet is to be preferred. It is manufactured from *Mucor miehei*, one of the mould group of fungi.

The Glue From Milk Experiment
Before we finish with milk I want to show you how to make an ancient form of glue. This was used by many ancient cultures including the ancient Egyptians and is still used to this day in woodworking and in gluing cardboard. It is a decent adhesive, although since it is made from animal protein it can in time go off.

REQUIREMENTS

✓ a bowl
✓ 2 pints of skimmed milk (you want to extract the protein casein, and you do not want the fat)
✓ 1 cup of white vinegar
✓ muslin cloth
✓ a sieve
✓ sodium bicarbonate

METHOD

Pour the milk into the bowl and add the vinegar. Then transfer this to a pan and gently heat, but do not let it boil. You will find that this causes the milk to separate out so that a solid material accumulates. Now sieve this through muslin, as you did in the cheese experiment to get the solid.

In a separate cup mix the sodium bicarbonate with a small amount of water, just enough to make a paste. Now gradually mix this with the curds until you have a white paste, like glue. Actually, it is glue!

EXPLANATION

As you know from earlier reading, casein is a protein in milk. It is basically acidic in nature. When you add the vinegar (acetic acid) to the milk you make it more acidic than the casein, so that it is displaced. The vinegar is acting as a demulsifier or emulsion-splitting agent and it separates out the solids (the casein in the curds) from the liquid (whey). By adding the sodium bicarbonate you are neutralizing the excess acid and producing the glue.

Now try it out.

CHAPTER FOUR

A DOZEN EGGSPERIMENTS

I love eggs, don't you? They really are quite fascinating things and there are lots of experiments that you will find fun to do. Some of these can be brushed up and performed as conjuring tricks to enhance your reputation as a wonder-worker. But don't ignore the science behind them.

THE ANATOMY OF AN EGG

An egg is a round or oval cell produced by the female of many, many species of creature. When it is fertilized by a reproductive cell from a male of the species then it can develop into an embryo, and thence through a multiplicity of changes into another individual of that species.

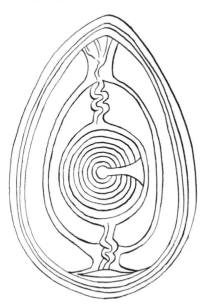

Eggs in the context of this chapter are hens' eggs. They are fairly typical of bird eggs and they are the commonest ones eaten by human beings. They are ovoid in shape, with a thin, hard shell, inside which is a membrane that contains the albumen or egg white. The yolk is suspended in the albumen by two strands of tissue called the chalazae. At the base of the egg is a large air sac.

1 The Silver Egg Experiment
You have heard of the goose that laid the golden egg. Well, here is how you can prepare a silver one.

REQUIREMENTS
✓ 1 hen's egg
✓ 1 candle

The internal anatomy of an egg

✓ a jam jar or glass of water
✓ 1 loop egg holder or a pair of forceps (this can be a bit messy)

METHOD

Light the candle and with the egg in the egg holder hold it in the candle flame and allow it to accumulate soot. It will do this quite quickly. Move the egg around so that eventually you have covered the whole shell in soot. It is important to get the whole shell covered. After allowing the egg to cool down, gently lower the egg into the jar of water so that it is completely submerged. *Et voila!* One silver egg.

EXPLANATION

This is simple optics. You have created an ovoid mirror effect. The carbon holds a layer of air so that the light is totally internally reflected and the egg will appear to have a silver surface. We will look at this phenomenon of total internal reflection in Chapter Eleven on A Little Light Relief.

2 The Boiled Egg Experiment

Do you know how to tell the difference between a fresh or raw egg and a boiled egg? This might come in useful one day when a boiled egg gets put back in the egg box by mistake.

The silver egg

REQUIREMENTS

✓ 2 eggs, 1 to be hard-boiled for up to 20 minutes, depending on size

METHOD

Quite simply, allow the boiled egg to settle to room temperature, just like the fresh egg. To tell them apart hold an egg by its long axis on a plate or a work surface and just spin each in turn. The fresh egg will spin slowly, whereas the boiled egg will spin fast. Once it exceeds about 10 revolutions a second it will probably even sit up and spin on its rounded end like a top.

EXPLANATION

This is all to do with rotational velocity. A raw egg has much of its mass in the form of a liquid, so it will move about as the egg is spun. It will not achieve its aimed-for rotational velocity. The boiled egg's proteins have become solids, so the egg achieves its rotational velocity and will spin fast.

3 The Egg In The Bottle Experiment

This is a good one to do after you have done the boiled egg experiment.

REQUIREMENTS

✓ 1 hardboiled egg
✓ 1 empty milk bottle (its aperture should be more than half the diameter of the egg, but the egg should be too big to slip into the bottle – you want it to look good, after all!)
✓ 3 matches

Show your grannie how to suck an egg!

METHOD

Peel the shell off the egg in readiness. Light the three matches and drop them into the bottle, letting them burn. Then straight away place the egg over the mouth of the bottle, thin end down. The flames will quickly go out and almost immediately you will see the egg appear to be sucked into the bottle.

EXPLANATION

The matches heat the air and cause it to expand so that some will be expelled from the bottle, and also the flame burns up the oxygen, so that there is less gas in the bottle. The egg seals the bottle and as the air that is left in the bottle cools down and contracts it will produce a vacuum-like effect. The pressure in the bottle will be less than the pressure outside so that the air pressure will force the egg into the bottle.

- And now for part two – getting the egg out of the bottle again. Well, you have a few options here:
- Turn the bottle upside down and blow hard into the bottle; this will cause air to enter the bottle. This pressure will 'blow' the egg out again
- Heat the bottle upside down under hot water. This will cause the air in the bottle to expand and push the egg out
- Drop an effervescent tablet inside with a little water, and then upend the bottle. The carbon dioxide produced will push the egg out
- Add a teaspoon of bicarbonate of soda and then a little vinegar. Upend the bottle and out it will come

Warning: this will produce a yukky egg. It is best to throw it away now. (See also Chapter Nine for the Unzip a Banana Experiment.)

4 The Bad Egg Experiment

A bad egg is one that has literally gone past its sell-by date. So how do you tell a fresh egg from a bad one?

REQUIREMENTS

✓ a few eggs of variable age
✓ a bowl of cold water

METHOD

The level of water in the bowl should be deep enough to cover an egg laid on its side by at least half an inch. A fresh egg will lie on its side at the bottom. An older egg that has not yet gone off will tilt up its rounded end. A bad egg will float.

EXPLANATION

Look at the cross section of an egg. The air pocket at the rounded end gets bigger the less fresh the egg. So a fresh egg is least buoyant and stays at the bottom, the bad egg is more buoyant and floats.

5 The Naked Egg Experiment

OK, it is time to introduce a little chemistry. This really is an old classic, but it leads on to a number of neat little experiments that you will want to try out. But study this one because the principle is interesting.

How to undress an egg and make it naked ...

REQUIREMENTS

✓ A tall jar
✓ Vinegar
✓ A fresh egg

METHOD

Immerse the egg in the jar and cover with vinegar. The first thing you will notice is that after a few minutes bubbles form around the egg. This is carbon dioxide being formed. Now put the jar in a fridge and leave for 24 hours.

When the time is up pour away this old vinegar and replace it with fresh. Put it back in the fridge and leave it for a week.

When you remove it, pour away the vinegar and gently wash it in cold water. The shell will have dissolved away completely, leaving a translucent, 'naked' egg. Put a torch behind it and see it trans-illuminate quite beautifully.

EXPLANATION

The shell of an egg is made up of:

calcium carbonate ($CaCO_3$)	94%
calcium phosphate ($Ca_3(PO_4)_2$)	1%
magnesium carbonate ($MgCO_3$)	1%
various organic compounds	4%

The vinegar is a 4–5 per cent solution of acetic acid (CH_3COOH)

The acetic acid and the calcium carbonate form the predominant **acid-base chemical reaction**, which will dissolve the shell. What happens is that the calcium carbonate reacts with the acetic acid to produce calcium acetate and carbon dioxide and water. Thus carbon dioxide is released as the bubbles you saw originally.

Thus:

$$CaCO_3 + 2\ (CH_3COOH) = Ca(CH_3COO)_2 + H_2O + CO_2$$

calcium carbonate + acetic acid   = calcium acetate   +   water   +   carbon dioxide

This leaves the egg contained within its membrane, as in the diagram of the anatomy of the egg.

NB: A variant on the egg in the bottle experiment is to use a softened egg shell rather than a boiled egg. To do this just have the egg in the fridge for two days rather than a week. The shell will probably be soft enough to perform the experiment without bursting – but it may, so be warned. But, the interesting thing is that if you leave it in the bottle for another 24 hours the shell will probably harden again.

6 The Secret Message Experiment

How to surprise someone with a secret message in a hard-boiled egg! (But please note – this egg is to be shown as a curio. It is **not to be eaten**, since alum contains a small amount of aluminium.)

REQUIREMENTS

✓ 1 hard-boiled egg
✓ 1 teaspoon of vinegar
✓ ½ a teaspoon of alum powder (aluminium potassium sulphate) (This used to be used to pickle eggs, but is harder to obtain nowadays. Your dad may have an alum block which he uses after shaving. It is used as a styptic to staunch cuts. You can scrape a little off the side and it immediately turns into powder. Or, you will find a tube of it in most chemistry sets.)
✓ a fine paintbrush

METHOD

Having boiled the egg set it aside in readiness. Dissolve the alum in the vinegar – as much as will dissolve in it. Then write your message on the egg shell by dipping the paintbrush in the vinegar and alum solution. Allow it to dry, so that the writing on the shell will become invisible. When the shell is later peeled off, your message will be visible on the egg surface. Spooky!

EXPLANATION

The acetic acid partially dissolves some of the shell, enough to allow the alum to permeate through the shell and appear on the surface of the egg.

7 The Etched Egg Experiment

This is fun and you might consider it a useful way to decorate your egg for Easter rather than just painting it.

REQUIREMENTS

✓ 1 hard-boiled egg
✓ a wax crayon (or more if you want to write or pattern with different colours)
✓ a jar
✓ vinegar to cover an egg
✓ an old toothbrush or nailbrush

METHOD

Take the boiled and cooled-down egg and write or make whatever pattern you want on the shell. Do it thickly. Then place the egg in the jar and cover with vinegar. After an hour take it out and wash it. Brush the shell. You will find that the pattern is etched into the shell and stands out from its surface.

EXPLANATION

Our old friend the acetic acid has etched away the shell, leaving your beautiful artwork or calligraphy to stand out unharmed.

8 The Magical Appearing Egg Experiment

This is a magic trick that looks as if you have transformed a piece of wet tissue paper into a solid fresh egg. (I warn you, it takes a lot of preparation, so it might pay you to have several eggs on the go – if mum lets you!)

REQUIREMENTS

✓ a blown egg
✓ a jar
✓ vinegar

(In the bad old days people used to collect birds' eggs and blow out the yolk. You need to do this first to the hen's egg. Bore a small hole in both ends of a fresh egg. Then with the bottom hole of the egg over a bowl, blow through the top hole. The contents will eventually all come out through the bottom hole. This now needs to be left to dry out the membrane for a day.)

... AND THE REQUIREMENTS FOR THE TRICK

✓ the membrane of the egg
✓ a table tennis bat
✓ piece of tissue paper

✓ glass of water
✓ a raw egg with a white shell and a bowl

METHOD

Go through exactly the same procedure as you did for the Naked Egg Experiment. What you will find is that you end up with a sac made up of the egg membranes. Powder the membrane with talcum powder and keep it in a box with talc.

PERFORMANCE OF THE TRICK

Have the membrane lying on a table behind a box. The raw egg is there as well. The bowl is at the front of the table where the audience can see. Take the tissue paper, tear off a small piece and moisten it and crumple it into a small size, about the size of the egg membrane. As you reach for the table tennis bat substitute the tissue paper for the egg membrane. Then say something along the lines of: 'Ladies and gentlemen, I am now going to demonstrate a curious phenomenon by which this magic table tennis bat can do the most amazing transformation. Observe this tissue paper.'

And you start to gently knock the membrane up and down on the bat. As you do so it will inflate into a perfect egg shape. It will stay inflated long enough for you to catch it, put it down behind the box (or if you know how, you palm the egg and substitute it. The membrane will collapse and is easily concealed).

'And now ladies and gentlemen – behold!' As you crack the egg into the bowl prepare to bow and take your well-earned adulation.

But it will take practice.

Now that's magic!

This is quite obvious and I am sure that I do not need to tell you. The membrane is of course egg shaped and it inflates as you knock it up and down.

9 The Floating Egg Experiment
How to make an egg float ...

✓ a fresh egg
✓ a jug half-full with salt water
✓ more fresh tap water

Prepare your salt water by dissolving as much salt as you can in about half a pint of water. Pour this into a jug. You can test this with your egg. It should float near the top. Assuming that it does, remove it and then gently pour the fresh tap water into the jug. Now when you are ready to perform this experiment or trick, tell your audience that eggs usually sink in water. Then gently drop it in. It will sink until it hits the salt layer and there it will stay.

The egg will float on the unseen salt layer

10 *The Egg Balancing Experiment*

Eggs don't balance, unless you know how to make them. This is a trick, impure and simple! And there are two methods.

These both work best with a table cloth on the table in front of you. Firstly, challenge people to make an egg stand on end and watch them fail. Then you pour out a few grains of salt on the table cloth. Now just stand the egg on them and it will stay upright.

Secondly, beforehand put a small finger ring under the tablecloth and make sure you can find it unaided. To make your egg stand, just place it atop the concealed ring!

11 *The Atlas Egg Experiment*

Everyone thinks that egg shells are fragile. They are not, as you can demonstrate with this experiment.

REQUIREMENTS

✓ 4 half shells from used hard-boiled eggs. Trim them so that they have a flat edge
✓ a stack of books, like the works of William Shakespeare

METHOD

Put four half shells in position and stack the books on them. They will hold their weight without crumbling. Just like Atlas.

12 *The Egg Squeezing Experiment*

This goes with the last experiment, but this time use a fresh egg. Simply ask your strong friend to hold a fresh egg in his hand and gently start

The Atlas
Eggshells

squeezing, building up the pressure to break the egg. He won't be able to do it. And the reason is the architecture of the shell. It will, like a three-dimensional arch, distribute the pressure all over the shell rather than on any point. The egg is not fragile, it is strong. It can deal with pressures like this, but sudden changes will crack it.

CHAPTER FIVE

THE ELEMENTS

The devil may write text books of chemistry
because every few years, the whole thing changes.
Jöns Jacob Berzelius (1779–1848)

Chemistry is the science concerned with the composition, structure and properties of matter as well as the changes that take place in chemical reactions. It necessitates the study of the elements. The development of chemistry itself is therefore worth some consideration.

Humankind has always wondered about how the universe is made up. In the ancient world various cultures developed ideas about life, the other creatures that shared the environment and all of the physical substance that made up that environment. Not surprisingly, divine intervention according to the religious beliefs of the culture was thought to be involved.

THE PHILOSOPHERS OF CLASSICAL GREECE

The ancient Greeks were intensely interested in people and their place in the scheme of things. Empedocles (c490–430BC) was a citizen of Agrigentum, a Greek city in Sicily. He was the first person to put forward a theory about how everything was made and suggested that there were four basic elements. These were earth, air, fire and water. Everything was made up of them, even people. The different combinations accounted for the huge array of different substances.

He taught that whenever they were given the opportunity to do so, the constituent elements would try to get back to their source. And he suggested that the sources had natural positions, such that earth was at the centre of the world, water covered it, and was in turn covered by air, which had above it fire from the sun.

Thus, when you burned wood, the flames would always rise upwards, as if trying to get back to the sun; the ash would crumble and try to get back to the earth; the smoke, being air, would try to get back to the sky;

and any sap in the wood would run out and try to get back to the sea. Similarly, solid objects put in water, being mainly earth, would sink. Bubbles, being air, would rise in water, and rain would fall through the air to get back to water.

Plato (428–348BC), the great mathematician and philosopher, was the founder of the Academy in Athens. He was the first person actually to use the term 'the elements' in about 360BC. His concept was that each element existed as tiny particles of the four elements that Empedocles had proposed, but that they had the specific shapes of the known regular poly-hedra. These were: cube (earth), octahedron (air), tetrahedron (fire) and icosahedron (water). He felt that these shapes would be compatible with the qualities of the elements, since a 6-sided cube could stack into a solid structure, like earth; the 20-sided icosahedrons would slip and slide past each other like water; the sharp, spiky 4-sided tetrahedrons would sting like fire; and the 8-sided octahedrons would slip, slide and bounce off each other like air.

Aristotle (384–322BC), another great philosopher, poet and proto-scientist, studied under Plato and became personal tutor to Alexander the Great. He added a fifth element, calling it the 'ether', corresponding to the divine force that made up the heavens and which animated tissues to produce life itself. He suggested that this element was made up of particles shaped like the fifth of the regular polyhedra, the twelve-sided dodecahedron.

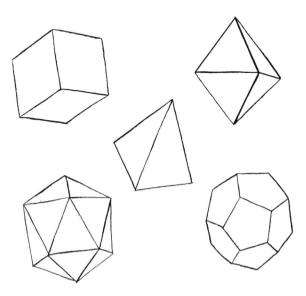

The Platonic solids

THE FIRST ATOMIC THEORY

Democritus (c460–370BC) was born in the city of Abdera in Thrace. He was a pupil of Leucippus, another philosopher, who is said to have developed an atomic theory. No one is clear about this – the records are sketchy – so Democritus has (rightly or wrongly) been given the accolade of coming up with the theory of atoms. Essentially, he disagreed with the element theory put forward by Empedocles and Plato and taught instead that all matter was made up of single types of particles called atoms. He envisaged these as being small spheres, which attached to others by means of hooks. He said that elements were composed only of one type of atom, and that other compounds were made of combinations of different types of atoms.

As you can imagine, this was a very different type of idea, not a million miles away from our modern atomic theories. The remarkable thing was that he came up with this hypothesis by pure reason, rather than through experimentation. Plato knew of Democritus's work and despised it, going so far as to wish that all of his books should be burned.

THE ALCHEMISTS

The ancient Egyptians and Mesopotamians practised alchemy. As such, they developed techniques to extract various elements and prepare metals. Since they were literate cultures their findings were all recorded in the Ancient Library of Alexandria, which is thought to have been founded in about 300BC. Its purpose was to accumulate all of the written lore of the world. Legend has it that Julius Caesar inadvertently burned it down when he set fire to ships in the Alexandria dock.

Various Arabian alchemists had absorbed that knowledge and developed the practice into a sort of proto-science. They believed that combinations of the four elements of Empedocles and Plato, plus **sulphur** and **mercury**, made up the various metals.

European alchemists in the Middle Ages continued in this belief and experimented with the various elements, especially the metals, in the hope of discovering the 'philosopher's stone', which would allow them to turn base metals into gold. In addition, they hoped that it would help them to discover the 'elixir of life'.

Alchemy was at this time a mix of rudimentary science, philosophy and magic, yet the alchemists did make some interesting discoveries. They developed the process of **distillation**, and discovered **sulphuric, nitric** and **hydrochloric acids, sodium bicarbonate**, as well as the elements **bismuth, arsenic, antimony** and **phosphorus**.

A handful of notable alchemists

Abu Musa Jabir (721–815), known by his Latinized name of Geber, was an Arabian physician, astrologer and alchemist. Some say he was the first to introduce true experimentation and the first to try to detach superstition from the practice of alchemy. He is famous for having discovered sulphuric, hydrochloric and nitric acids.

Nicolas Flamel (1330–1418) was a scrivener (essentially a literate clerk and manuscript copier) who became noted as an alchemist. He is said to have discovered the philosopher's stone and the elixir of life. His house at 51 rue de Montmorency still stands and is the oldest house in Paris. Curiously, his tomb is said to be empty and there are some who claim that he is still alive today, thanks to his discoveries. Readers of the Harry Potter books will be familiar with his name!

Theophrastus Philippus Aureolus Bombastus von Hohenheim (1493–1541), who became known to the world as Paracelsus, was a physician, alchemist, astrologer and occultist. He pioneered the use of minerals in medicine and is thought to have been the discoverer of **zinc**. He agreed with the Greek theory of the elements, but added his own concept that three additional controlling elements, sulphur, mercury and salt, in combination with them would give them their individual properties.

Johann Rudolf Glauber (1604–1670) was the son of a barber who became an apothecary and an alchemist. He made several extremely important contributions, including ways of preparing concentrated solutions of the three main acids that had been discovered by the Arabian alchemist Geber. In addition, in 1625 he discovered the chemical **sodium sulphate**, which he called *sal mirabilis*, meaning 'wonderful salt'. He discovered that it had a marked laxative effect (helps the bowels work), so it was used medicinally. Indeed, it was the most effective laxative in use until the twentieth century. Subsequently, it was called Glauber's salt after him, a name that it retains to this day. His discoveries are really quite important, so we shall meet him again in the next chapter.

Hennig Brand (1630–1710) was a merchant and alchemist in Hamburg. In 1669 he discovered the element **phosphorus** by heating residues from boiled-down urine in a furnace until the retort grew red hot. His reason for doing this was because he thought that the gold colour of urine might be a clue in his search for a means of producing gold. What he did find was that the retort filled with glowing fumes and liquid dripped out, bursting into flames immediately. He collected the liquid in a jar and covered it, where it solidified and continued to give off a pale-green glow. What he had collected was phosphorus, which he named from the Greek words meaning 'light-bearer'.

It is one of the bitter ironies of history that during the Second World War the city of Hamburg, where Brand had discovered phosphorus, was extensively and devastatingly bombed with phosphorus-containing bombs.

ROBERT BOYLE: THE SCEPTICAL CHYMIST

Robert Boyle (1627–1691) is one of the most important people in the history of science. He was born into wealth as the seventh son and the fourteenth child of Richard Boyle, the First Earl of Cork.

Boyle was educated at Eton after which he embarked on the Grand Tour, as did so many of the wealthy aristocracy of his day. In 1641 he visited Florence in Italy, where the aged Galileo Galilei was still living under house arrest by order of the Inquisition. Boyle and his tutor spent that winter in Florence studying the works of Galileo. When Galileo died the following year Boyle felt stimulated to study astronomy and science.

Boyle made many discoveries in his career, across the whole range of science. He was the first person to demonstrate that air was necessary for combustion to take place, that animals needed it to breathe, and that it was needed for the transmission of sound. With a colleague, Robert Hooke (1635–1703), he built a vacuum pump. His most famous discovery is enshrined in Boyle's Law, which he formulated in 1662. This states that *at constant temperature* for a fixed mass, the absolute pressure and the volume of a gas are inversely proportional.

He did many alchemical experiments in his laboratory, coming to the conclusion that the old Greek theories about the elements, and those of Paracelsus, were absolutely incorrect. He expressed all this in his book *The Sceptical Chymist* in 1661. It is widely regarded as the point where science detached itself from alchemy and is the first book of chemistry.

Hooke theorized that the elements were made up of 'corpuscles' of varying sizes, which could mix and combine to produce compounds. He demonstrated in his experiments that compounds had very different properties from those of the constituent elements.

And of relevance to the next experiment that you may like to try out, Robert Boyle was the inventor of the match, in 1680!

THE HISTORY OF THE MATCH

In 1669 the alchemist Hennig Brand discovered phosphorus by heating urine and water. In 1680 the scientist Robert Boyle coated paper with phosphorus and wood with suphur. Friction between them caused fire and the principle of the match was invented. In 1827 the apothecary John Walker coated small slivers of wood with antimony sulphide, potassium chlorate, gum and starch and let them dry. These could then be struck on any solid surface to produce a flame. This was the first commercial match.

And this must be a good point to do an experiment. See if you have learned anything.

The Smoking And Glowing Fingers Experiment!

Are you brave enough to see your fingers produce smoke and glow in the dark?

REQUIREMENTS

✓ a box of safety matches
✓ a tin plate or lid of a can that you have cooled down in a fridge
✓ a finger and thumb (the ones you snap with will do perfectly well)

METHOD

Cut the striker surface off the box and bend it in half and stand it like a tent, striker surface facing downwards, on top of the cold plate. Then light it so that burns. This will only take about a minute. You will find that it just crinkles up and then goes out. There shouldn't be much ash. Just set the striker aside and look underneath. You will find a rather unappealing brown residue on the cold plate.

Now for the exciting bit. Rub the pulps of your finger and thumb in the residue and get a slight coating on them (most people snap with their thumb and middle finger). Now snap them two or three times. As you straighten them out you will see smoke coming from them.

And if you do this at night and switch off the lights you will see your finger and thumb have a slight greenish glow for a moment or two. Spooky!

The smoking and glowing fingers experiment

EXPLANATION

The secret is all in the nature of safety matches. And we need just to look at this first. Safety matches were first produced because a match was needed that did not self-combust. They have to be struck against a special surface to cause them to ignite. The match contains the element **sulphur**, often as the chemical compound antimony sulphide, ground glass, together with oxidizing agents such as potassium chlorate, powdered glass and various binding agents. The striking surface consists of powdered glass or silica, **red phosphorus**, and again various binding agents. When you strike the match against the striker the friction of glass against glass produces heat, which converts the red phosphorus into **white phosphorus** vapour. This ignites spontaneously and causes the potassium chlorate to decompose and liberate oxygen. This causes the sulphur to burn and – bingo – the wooden match is lit!

Now that you understand the science, what about the spooky glow and the smoke? Well, the residue contains both potassium salts and a compound of phosphorus. When you rub it against the finger and thumb, or snap your fingers, you again produce heat and release **potassium pentoxide**. You will be aware of a garlicky odour at the same time. Potassium pentoxide fumes cause the smoke and, while the reaction is still going on, it glows green.

> **CAUTION**
>
> This is not an experiment to perform repeatedly, since phosphorus salts can be absorbed through the skin. But just wash the residue off after the experiment and all will be well.

Now: back to some history!

JOHN DALTON AND THE ATOMIC THEORY

John Dalton (1766–1844) was born into a Quaker family. It is amazing for us to imagine the difficulties that one's religious persuasion could create, but his beliefs prevented him from following a career in law or medicine, both of which he had considered, because 'dissenters' were not permitted to attend English universities in those days. Fortunately, New College in Manchester had been set up especially for dissenters and he moved there in 1793 to teach mathematics and physics.

Dalton is most famous for his work on gases and for the development of the Atomic Theory. His Atomic Theory states that:

- All matter is composed of atoms
- Atoms cannot be made or destroyed
- All atoms of the same element are identical
- Different elements have different types of atoms
- Chemical reactions occur when atoms are rearranged
- Compounds are formed from the atoms of the constituent elements

John Dalton was a scientific genius, albeit an erratic experimenter. One reason for his erraticism is that he suffered from colour blindness, and was the first person to describe the condition. It was named Daltonism in his honour.

BERZELIUS AND THOSE WONDERFUL CHEMICAL FORMULAE

Jöns Jacob Berzelius (1779–1848) was a Swedish chemist who devised the chemical formulae that we use today. These dramatically simplified the expression of chemistry and of chemical reactions. He also introduced various chemical terms, such as catalyst, polymer and isomer.

While working on a textbook he discovered the **law of constant proportions**. Effectively this means that inorganic compounds are composed of constant proportions of the different elements by weight. It provided evidence in support of John Dalton's Atomic Theory.

He discovered the elements **cerium, silicon, selenium** and **thorium** and was influential in the discovery of **lithium** and **vanadium**.

MENDELEEV AND THE PERIODIC TABLE

Dmitri Ivanovich Mendeleev (1834–1907) was a Russian chemist and inventor who formulated the Periodic Table of the Elements. This is the blueprint for the whole of chemistry.

Since the 1860s various chemists had been working on a way of systemizing the elements, since various elements seemed to have properties in common. For example, Johann Döbereiner in 1817 formulated his **law of triads**, in which he stated that each triad contained three elements with similar properties. Thus the elements lithium, potassium and sodium were alkali producers, while chlorine, bromine and iodine were salt formers. John Newlands, an English chemist, in 1861 noticed other properties and introduced his **law of octaves**. He had noticed that every eighth element had similar characteristics and properties and arranged the known elements at the time in groups of eight.

Mendeleev built on all this to produce a table of the elements that showed that if the elements were arranged in ascending atomic weight and arranged in regard to their properties, then you could actually predict missing elements. The legend is that he had been working on the idea for so long that he grew obsessed with it. One night, he dreamed of playing cards, and laid out the cards in a periodic manner, each card representing an element.

GROUPS

		1	2	3	4	5	6	7	8	9	10	11	12	13	14	15	16	17	18
	1	1 H																	2 He
P E R I O D S	2	3 Li	4 Be											5 B	6 C	7 N	8 O	9 F	10 Ne
	3	11 Na	12 Mg											13 Al	14 Si	15 P	16 S	17 Cl	18 Ar
	4	19 K	20 Ca	21 Sc	22 Ti	23 V	24 Cr	25 Mn	26 Fe	27 Co	28 Ni	29 Cu	30 Zn	31 Ga	32 Ge	33 As	34 Se	35 Br	36 Kr
	5	37 Rb	38 Sr	39 Y	40 Zr	41 Nb	42 Mo	43 Tc	44 Ru	45 Rh	46 Pd	47 Ag	48 Cd	49 In	50 Sn	51 Sb	52 Te	53 I	54 Xe
	6	55 Cs	56 Ba	71 Lu	72 Hf	73 Ta	74 W	75 Re	76 Os	77 Ir	78 Pt	79 Au	80 Hg	81 Tl	82 Pb	83 Bi	84 Po	85 At	86 Rn
	7	87 Fr	88 Ra	103 Lr	104 Rf	105 Db	106 Sg	107 Bh	108 Hs	109 Mt	110 Ds	111 Rg	112 Uub	113 Uut	114 Uuq	115 Uup	116 Uuh	117 Uus	118 Uuo

6	57 La	58 Ce	59 Pr	60 Nd	61 Pm	62 Sm	63 Eu	64 Gd	65 Tb	66 Dy	67 Ho	68 Er	69 Tm	70 Yb
7	89 Ac	90 Th	91 Pa	92 U	93 Np	94 Pu	95 Am	96 Cm	97 Bk	98 Cf	99 Es	100 Fm	101 Md	102 No

The Periodic Table

The Periodic Table of the Elements is arranged in horizontal rows and vertical columns. The elements are placed according to increasing **atomic number**.[4]

The horizontal rows are called 'periods' and the vertical columns are called 'groups'. Each group represents a shared family of elements, all with similar appearance, properties and reactivity.

Thus Group 1 (apart from hydrogen) represents the alkali metals, lithium, sodium, potassium and so on to francium. They are all silvery coloured, highly reactive metals. The next group is the alkaline earth metals, from beryllium, magnesium and calcium through to radium. These are also highly reactive. Then there is the block of transition metals, which are all strong with high melting and boiling points. The groups 14, 15 and 16 are mainly composed of the non-metals. Group 17 are the non-metal halogens, which are highly reactive. Group 18 shows the noble gases, which are the least reactive of all.

The lanthanides, or rare earth metals (atomic numbers 57–71), the upper of the two bottom periods (horizontal rows), are all so similar in their chemical character that they are all placed in the same space in the table, number 57. Similarly, the actinides, or the rare earth radioactive metals, are all placed in the same place: 89.

You now have a pretty good idea of the Periodic Table.

NAMES IN THE PERIODIC TABLE

You might find it an interesting exercise (or not) to see if you can work out why the elements got their names. For instance, there are ten famous scientists lurking there. These are:

Bohrium, symbol **Bh**, atomic number 107, named after Niels Bohr (1885–1927), theoretical physicist famous for quantum mechanics

Curium, symbol **Cm**, atomic number 96, named after Marie Curie (1867–1934), physicist famous for the discovery of radioactivity

Einsteinium, symbol **Es**, atomic number 99, named after Albert Einstein (1879–1955), theoretical physicist famous for the Theory of Relativity

Fermium, symbol **Fm**, atomic number 100, named after Enrico Fermi (1901–1954), physicist famous for his work on particle physics and the development of the nuclear reactor

Gadolinium, symbol **Gd**, atomic number 64, named after Johan Gadolin (1760–1852), Finnish chemist and geologist famous for discovering **yttrium,** the first rare earth metal to be discovered

Mendelevium, symbol **Md**, atomic number 101, named after Dmitri Mendeleev (1834–1907), chemist famous for the Periodic Table of the Elements

Nobelium, symbol **No**, atomic number 102, named after Alfred Nobel (1833–1896), famous for the invention of dynamite and for donating his fortune to establish the Nobel Prize

Roentgenium, symbol **Rg**, Atomic number 111, named after Wilhelm Conrad Röntgen (1845–1923), physicist famous for the discovery of X-rays

Rutherfordium, symbol **Rf**, Atomic number 104, named after Ernest Rutherford (1871–1937), famous for splitting the atom

Seaborgium, symbol **Sg**, Atomic number 106, named after Glenn T Seaborg (1912–1999), famous for his discovery of several of the actinides

CARBON

Carbon, symbol C, atomic number 6, is a member of group 14. It is the fourth most abundant element in the universe and the fifteenth most abundant in the earth's crust. It has been known about since antiquity, the name coming from the Latin *carba*, meaning 'coal'.

Carbon is incredibly versatile, forming over 10 million compounds. It is studied in inorganic chemistry, and the hydrocarbons and their derivatives are studied in organic chemistry.

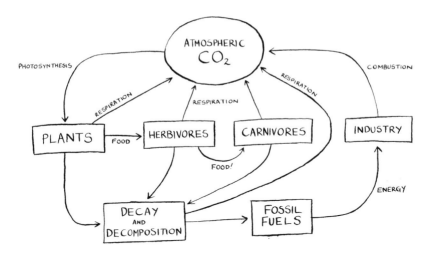

The Carbon Cycle

The carbon cycle

This is extremely important for everyone to know about. When I was learning science at school the carbon cycle was a useful little diagram to learn for tests, but now it is vital that people absorb its meaning if the world is to survive!

We all need to take steps to reduce our carbon footprint.

Organic chemistry and the snake that swallowed its tail

Prang, our chemistry teacher, used to tell us that organic chemistry was a dream subject and that we should all feel privileged to study it. He told us that the whole subject was in fact based on a dream.

The dream took place in 1865 and the dreamer was a chemistry professor by the name of Friedrich August Kekulé (1829–1896). He had been studying the nature of carbon and the way that carbon bonds were formed for so long that he began seeing them in his dreams. One particular daydream resulted in him seeing a snake eating its own tail. This image clicked with him and he realized how carbon atoms must join together to produce benzene.[5] Thus the benzene ring was described as a six carbon ring with alternating single and double bonds. This insight saw an amazing development in chemistry and virtually created the whole discipline of organic chemistry.

Even Father Christmas needs to watch his carbon footprints!

In 1895 Kekulé was ennobled by Kaiser Wilhelm II of Germany. Three of his students were subsequently awarded the Nobel Prize for Chemistry.

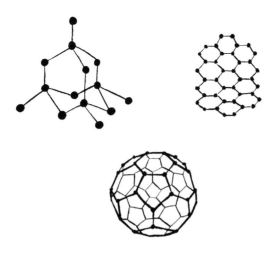

Diamond,
Graphite and the
'Buckyball'

The different forms of carbon

Allotropy is the name for different forms of an element. Carbon has several allotropes, which demonstrate how one element can have very different properties depending upon the way its atoms relate to one another. **Graphite**, which is used in pencils, is grey and soft because its atoms are arranged in layers of regular hexagons which 'slide' over one another. **Amorphous carbon** has no crystalline structure but is reactive carbon compacted together. It occurs as coal and soot and is black. **Diamond** is the hardest natural substance and when pure is colourless and transparent. Its atoms are arranged in a three-dimensional network arranged tetrahedrally in space.

The next lot of allotropes were not known about until they were described in 1985 by a team from Rice University in Houston and the University of Sussex.[6] These are the **Buckminsterfullerenes**, usually just known as the fullerenes, and are molecules of carbon that form into hollow structures. There are three shapes that have been described – a sphere, an ellipsoid and a tube. The sphere is known as the 'buckyball'. It was the first to be discovered and described and in full is called **buckminster-fullerene** or C_{60}. They all have a similar stacking, like graphite.

The significance of these hollow molecules is staggering, because it is not inconceivable that they could be 'filled' and used in medicine and all manner of nano-technology. To get an idea of the shape of a buckyball, you just have to think of a modern football design.

The Davy lamp

I worked as a family doctor in Yorkshire for almost 30 years. When I first arrived at my workplace it was quite clear that it was a mining town. There were several collieries within it, with their great black heaps of coal and their awesome pit wheels. I felt it was a privilege to look after so many miners and their families. When I retired I was given a Davy lamp, such as they used to use. It is one of my most treasured possessions. I mention it here because my old chemistry teacher Prang had impressed the importance of its invention upon us all those years before. I feel that it is also symbolic of carbon, coal and mining.

This invention was the brainchild of Sir Humphry Davy (1778–1829) in 1815. It is a miner's safety lamp consisting of a wick and oil container. Davy had discovered that a flame enclosed inside a fine mesh does not ignite methane, or 'firedamp', as the miners knew it. The mesh screen acts as a flame arrestor. This means that although air and other gases, including methane, could pass through the mesh and be combusted, the holes were too fine to allow a flame to propagate through them in the other direction to ignite a concentration of methane outside. It was a fantastically simple invention of amazing potential to save lives. Until then miners had used

My Davy Lamp

candles to work by, and took canaries down mines with them, since they were particularly sensitive to methane, and their distress would alert miners to the presence of the gas.

Not only was the lamp a safety against methane and other gases, but it gave miners a crude test for the presence of gases. If flammable gases like methane were present the flame flared blue and burned higher than usual. If on the other hand there was a build up of oxygen-poor air, or 'chokedamp' as it was called (essentially air that was deficient in oxygen and which had a build up of dense carbon dioxide and other gases), then the flame would be reduced and could go out. The test was to place the lamp on the ground where the dense gases would accumulate. If a miner stayed long in such conditions he could asphyxiate and be overcome.

Sir Humphrey Davy uses electrolysis to discover a host of elements

Potassium, symbol K, atomic number 19, is a member of group 1. It was among several elements discovered by Sir Humphry Davy during his career. In 1807 he isolated it by the electrolysis of very dry molten caustic potash (KOH, potassium hydroxide). It was the first metal isolated by electrolysis.

Sodium, symbol Na, atomic number 11, is another member of group 1. This he also discovered by the electrolysis of caustic soda (NaOH) in 1807. Calcium, symbol Ca, atomic number 20, group 2, was next to be discovered by Davy when he electrolyzed a mixture of lime and mercuric oxide. In later years, by the same method, he discovered barium, boron and magnesium.

Sadly, it is likely that this genius may have died early, at the age of 50, after a lifetime of handling and inhaling dangerous chemicals.

NITROGEN

Nitrogen, symbol N, atomic number 7, group 15, is a gas that makes up 78 per cent of the earth's atmosphere. We don't really use it in this form, but it is vital for life. We absorb it from the food chain.

Nitrogen was discovered in 1772 by Professor Daniel Rutherford (1749–1819), a Scottish chemist and physician. He called it 'phlogisticated air'. This was because the phlogiston theory was the flavour of science at the time. If you want to read more on this, then go to the next chapter, Now For Some Fizzics, where we look at oxygen and consider the phlogiston theory in some detail.

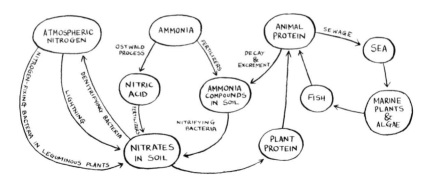

The Nitrogen Cycle

We spent forever going through the nitrogen cycle when I was at school, so here it is to remind you.

IRON

Iron, symbol Fe, atomic number 26, group 8, is a transition metal. The earth is mainly just a great chunk of iron, while Mars is red because most of its surface may be rust.

Iron filings make great oofle dust!

Your mum might have some iron cooking utensils. It is a great conductor of heat. It doesn't occur much in nature as the pure element, but has to be extracted from minerals. Lodestone is the name for a magnetic iron compound called magnetite, which is magnetizable. The ancients used it to make compasses.

As iron filings it makes great oofle dust! Just drop a pinch on top of a candle and see it sparkle and fizz. And that is a good point to look at a bit of fizzics.

CHAPTER SIX

NOW FOR SOME FIZZICS
... OR, THINGS THAT FIZZ

We saw in the last chapter that the alchemists discovered sulphuric, nitric and hydrochloric acids. Until that time the only acid used had been vinegar. And what a wonderful thing vinegar is. It is probably one of the very first cooking ingredients, and almost certainly one of the first chemicals that humans ever used.

ACIDS

Most ancient cultures used vinegar. A jar found in the Middle East dating back to 8,000BC was used to contain vinegar, and Egyptian papyri from 3,000BC tell of its use as an antiseptic in medicine. According to legend, Queen Cleopatra dissolved pearls in vinegar to prove that she could

The Volcano
experiment

consume a fortune in a single meal. The Babylonians fermented date palm juice to produce vinegar, which they used as a preservative agent, which would have been of inestimable value in those hot, hazy days when food would go off so quickly. The Chinese also were using it in ancient times, as its use is recorded in a textbook of medicine from 2,000BC.

It was the Greeks who first described vinegar in a chemical sense, when they noted that it was capable of 'eating' or corroding certain things, as well as being able to preserve foods. The Romans, who absorbed so much of Greek knowledge, called it *vinum acetum*, which is Latin for 'sour wine'. This ultimately became transformed into French as *vin aigre*, which in English became 'vinegar'.

Fruit juices can, if left, become tainted with micro-organisms that ferment their sugar to produce alcohol:

Glucose $\rightarrow$ carbon dioxide + ethyl alcohol + energy
$C_6H_{12}O_6$ $\rightarrow$ $2CO_2 + 2C_2H_5OH$ + energy

Under further microbial action the ethyl alcohol that is formed, and the ethyl alcohol in wine or beer, is oxidized to produce acetic acid.[7]

Ethyl alcohol + oxygen $\rightarrow$ Acetic acid + water
C_2H_5OH $+ O_2$ $\rightarrow$ CH_3COOH + H_2O

This sour taste of fruit juices or wine that had gone off to produce vinegar became used to characterize the group of liquids that had these useful properties. Thus the Latin word *acidus*, meaning 'sour-tasting', became shortened to 'acid'.

As we saw in the last chapter, Johann Rudolf Glauber discovered *sal mirabilis* (sodium sulphate, Na_2SO_4). But he also developed methods of concentrating the three powerful acids that had first been identified by Geber. These concentrated forms were much more powerful and much more effective than the types previously available. They were also a significant advance on vinegar in alchemical experiments. He called these *spiritus salis* (hydrochloric acid, HCl), *vitriol* (sulphuric acid, H_2SO_4) and *spiritus acidus nitri* (nitric acid, HNO_3).

These powerful acids proved to be a way of obtaining precious metals such as gold and silver, which were often combined as alloys. It was found that powerful acids like sulphuric and nitric acid could dissolve the silver. They were seen as being metal purifiers. And that was only the start of their usefulness.

ALKALIS

The ancient Greeks were also aware of another group of substances that had a use, but which were quite different from vinegar. These all have a slimy or slippery feel. They were left as a residue when certain things were burned. These were called potash, (potassium carbonate, K_2CO_3), produced from wood ash; soda, (sodium hydroxide, NaOH) from boiling certain liquids away; and lime (Calcium oxide, CaO), produced from burning sea shells.

These substances were representatives of a group composed of either the hydroxide or the carbonate of an alkaline metal (see last chapter about the Periodic Table). They seemed to have an ability to clean things and be able to dissolve the element sulphur and various oils.

They came to be known as the 'alkalis', from the Arabic word *al-qaliy*, meaning 'the calcined ashes'. Generally, the alkalis are easily dissolved in water. You will find them around the house in the form of detergents, bleach and cleaning agents.

THE SALTS

It had been noted by alchemists that certain combinations of substances produced very marked reactions. Johann Rudolf Glauber decided to study this and found that acids and alkalis reacted often quite violently with each other to produce a fizzing effect, or effervescence.

After a major experiment that he performed in 1658 he wrote that when *nitri fixi* (potash or potassium carbonate, one of the alkalis) is added to *spiritus nitri* (nitric acid) they effectively 'have a battle and slay one another'. By this he meant that they neutralized one another. Yet he also made one of the most significant discoveries of all, for they also produced another type of substance: a salt.

When Glauber added sulphuric acid to ordinary salt, sodium chloride, he found that a completely new salt was produced. This was *sal mirabilis* (sodium sulphate, Na_2SO_4), known ever after as Glauber's salt.

Glauber had made his contribution, and then it was back over to Robert Boyle.

INDICATORS

Robert Boyle was very interested in Glauber's work on salts. Indeed, he saw that the formation of salts supported his theories about the nature of the elements (see the last chapter) and made the old theory about the four elements seem less plausible.

Boyle did many experiments on acids, alkalis and salts and came to the conclusion, as had Glauber, that acids and alkalis neutralized each other, often by producing effervescence, and produced a salt and water in the process.

Here are examples of three acids reacting with sodium hydroxide:

$$HCl + NaOH \rightarrow NaCl + H_2O$$
$$HNO_3 + NaOH \rightarrow NaNO_3 + H_2O$$
$$H_2SO_4 + 2NaOH \rightarrow Na_2SO_4 + 2H_2O$$

Boyle was interested in determining how you could distinguish acids from alkalis other than by tasting for acids (which is not sensible for strong acids) or by assessing their slipperiness for alkalis. He was aware that French dyers used various plant juices to dye silks, and that they could alter their colours by adding various substances. These substances turned out to be acids and alkalis.

Boyle published a book in 1664, entitled *Experimental History of Colours*. In this he described his experiments in this area and his conclusions. He found that if acid was added to purple plant juice it would turn it red. If an alkali was added instead, then the juice would turn bluish-green.

He had discovered the principle of indicators. He worked with many of these in solutions, but now introduced one of the most useful aids to chemistry – litmus paper. You will have used it many times in the school lab.

Boyle produced this by soaking small strips of paper in lichen[8] juice and then dried them out to produce a purple paper. When this was dipped in acid it would turn red and when dipped in alkali it would go blue or blue–green.

And now it is time to do a few little experiments.

Natural Indicator Experiments
It is quite remarkable how many plants can be used as natural indicators. Try these out.

REQUIREMENTS
✓ 3 test tubes and test tube rack or 3 small glasses, to be used for each of the following:
✓ turmeric or curry powder
✓ cold tea
✓ blackberry juice
✓ red cabbage leaves
✓ onion
Also, when available, try the following flowers:
✓ delphinium

✓ geranium
✓ hollyhocks
✓ petunia
✓ violets
plus:
✓ clear vinegar
✓ sodium bicarbonate powder
✓ blotting paper

METHOD

For the red cabbage chop up two or three leaves then boil in half a cup of water for ten minutes. Strain the liquid into a jug and allow it to cool. It should be blue–purple in colour. When it is cold pour about an inch into the three test tubes. The middle one is to be the neutral comparison. Now add a teaspoon of vinegar to the first one and note how it changes to red. Then into the third tube add a pinch of sodium bicarbonate. It should change to blue.

You don't need to boil fruit juices, they tend to colour well. Make tea as you usually would. For the turmeric or curry powder use about a teaspoon in half a cup of water.

You will find that in acid tea goes pale and in alkali it goes very dark. Turmeric goes yellow in acid and orange in alkali, dark fruits and vegetables go red in acid and blue in alkali. Onion tends to be a neutral colour in acid (except red onion will be slightly red in acid) and green in alkali.

To test the flowers, just put a petal in the three cleaned test tubes.

You can also use blotting paper, as Boyle did, to create alkali and acid indicators from a fruit juice like blackberry. Simply soak strips of blotting paper in the freshly prepared juice and let them dry. This is an alkali indicator – it will go blue in alkali solution. And to prepare an acid indicator, take some of the juice and add sodium bicarbonate to it until in changes blue. Then soak fresh blotting paper strips in it and let them dry. These are acid indicators, which go red in acid solution.

So go on, have a go and devise your own experiments so that you can start testing household products. But be careful with alkaline substances and do experiments near a sink. If any spill on to the skin then wash off with copious amounts of cold water.

EXPLANATION

There are four groups of pigments in leaves. These include the chlorophylls, the carotenoids, anthrocyanins and anthoanthins. The anthrocyanins are the ones that react most to changes in acidity and alkalinity and produce the red in acid, blue in alkali colour changes that we have found so useful in the dying industry and in chemistry.

TEST TUBE EXPERIMENTS AND LIVING TESTS

Certain growing flowers exhibit colour changes according to the acid content of the soil. This is used by growers to predict the colour and hues of blooms. *Hydrangea microphylla* is the plant used most commonly to do this, and it produces blue flowers in acid soils and pink flowers in alkaline soil.

That's right – blue in acid and pink in alkali, the opposite from all of the test tube tests. This is often the case with *in vitro* tests, meaning that test tube or laboratory tests do not always match up with *in vivo* tests, or experiments carried out with living systems. In this case it is because the colour change actually is all about making aluminium available to the plant. Acid soils enhance its availability and alkaline ones reduce it.

This is a valuable point. Remember it!

pH – a measure of acidity and alkalinity

In 1909 the Danish chemist Søren Peder Lauritz Sørensen introduced a means of measuring the range of acidity and alkalinity. You may be amazed to know it, but it is not clear today exactly what the 'p' in pH stands for, although it is said that Sørensen intended it to stand for the 'Power of Hydrogen'. It is a mathematical measure that is defined as the co-logarithm of the activity of dissolved hydrogen ions (H^+).

For your interest, this can be written as:

$$pH = -\log_{10}(a_H+) = \log_{10}\left(\frac{1}{a_H+}\right)$$

where a_H is the (dimensionless) activity of hydrogen ions.

What you need to know is that the scale of pH runs from 0 to 14, with acids being the lowest, distilled water being neutral at 7 and alkalis increasing in strength to 14.

pH of Common Substances

Battery acid	1
Stomach acid (HCl)	1–2
Lemon juice	1–2
Vinegar	2–3
Milk	6.5–7
Distilled water	7
Sodium bicarbonate	8
Milk of Magnesia (stomach antacid)	10
Household bleach	12.5

Other indicators

There are many other indicators that are used in the laboratory. The common ones apart from litmus are phenolphthalein, methyl red, methyl orange, methyl violet and universal indicator. The latter was first patented in 1923 and changes colour through the spectrum from red to purple.

pH Range	Description	Colour
0–3	Strong acid	Red
3–6	Acid	Orange/Yellow
7	Neutral	Green
8–11	Base	Blue
11–14	Strong base	Purple

Effervescence – the fizz factor

Effervescence is the release of a gas from an aqueous solution. If you mix vinegar or lemon juice and sodium bicarbonate, you will produce a nice fizzing foam as the acid and base (alkali) react to produce carbon dioxide. Carbon dioxide is the fizz factor in many things that you come across. We came across it in the bread-making experiment and the leavening agent experiment in Chapter Two on Cooking Chemistry.

To recap, the reaction is:

$$NaHCo3 \quad + \quad H^+ \quad \rightarrow \quad Na^+ \quad + \quad CO_2 \quad + \quad H_2O$$

Carbon dioxide was first discovered in the 1750s by Joseph Black (1728–1799), a Scottish doctor and chemist. He found that when lime-stone was heated or treated with strong acids it produced a gas that he called 'fixed air'. He found that this gas was heavier than air, that it did not support combustion (it put out candles and flames – see Chapter Two) and that it did not support animal life. Further, he found that it was given off during fermentation and during animal respiration.

Joseph Priestley (1733–1804) was an English chemist, theologian and natural philosopher. He performed major work on gases, including carbon dioxide, and was the discoverer of oxygen – although he called it **dephlogisticated air** – as well as being an innovator in the field of electricity and optics.

In 1772 Priestley published a pamphlet entitled *Directions for Impregnating Water with Fixed Air* in which he described how to produce soda water by dissolving carbon dioxide in water. He had thought, incorrectly as we now know, that soda water might prevent sailors from getting scurvy.[9] Although this became the basis for all carbonated drinks, Priestley failed to patent the method and so gained no financial benefit from his discovery.

The Volcano Experiment

This effervescence always looks impressive, especially if you have a younger brother or sister.

REQUIREMENTS

✓ play dough or clay
✓ vinegar
✓ sodium bicarbonate
✓ food colouring

METHOD

Construct a volcano out of play dough or clay and place it on a tray. Perhaps make it about the size of your fist. Make sure that you have given it a base, so that it is essentially like a small bottle inside. Drop a couple of teaspoons of bicarbonate of soda powder into the hollow. You can also, if you wish, add and mix two or three drops of food colouring – but if so, make sure that the volcano is on a tray and not on a table top where it could stain!

When you are ready, drop some 'acid rain' (vinegar or lemon juice) into the volcano and watch it erupt. It will effervesce and keep effervescing until the reaction is complete.

EXPLANATION

Do I really need to tell you?

The Lemonade Experiment

How about a little carbonization?

REQUIREMENTS

✓ 1 lemon
✓ 1 pint of water
✓ 1 teaspoon of sugar
✓ 1 half teaspoon of sodium bicarbonate

METHOD

Slice the lemon up and boil it in water for 10 minutes. Once it is cool strain the liquid into a jug. Add the sugar and mix it up. When you are ready to drink it simply pour a glass and add the sodium bicarbonate and give a stir. It will fizz and you have one delicious glass of lemonade.

EXPLANATION

Oh, come on!

The Sherbet-Making Experiment

Right, so you have made your own lemonade. Now, why not try your hand at making your own sherbet? If you tell your dad about it he will probably go all misty eyed and think of those tubes of sherbet with a liquorice straw in the end that looked like a stick of dynamite. You bit the end off the liquorice and used it as a straw to suck up a mouthful of sherbet powder, which would immediately fizz in your mouth. Not so great for the teeth, though, since it is full of sugar. But with that proviso, why not try the sherbet-making experiment?

REQUIREMENTS

- ✓ 2 teaspoons of icing sugar
- ✓ 1 teaspoon of citric acid powder – or tartaric acid powder
- ✓ ½ teaspoon of sodium bicarbonate powder
- ✓ a hollow liquorice stick (optional)

METHOD

On a plate mix the three ingredients to form the powder. And that's it! You have actually created sherbet. You can if you wish suck some up through a liquorice straw, but that isn't necessary. The sweet manufacturers just did that to give the sherbet some flavour. The thing is that when you wet this powder, with the saliva in your mouth, it will fizz. You may need to juggle a bit with the quantities to get the right taste, but that is the basic method and the correct ratio of 2:1:0.5 for sugar:citric acid:sodium bicarbonate

Then – brush your teeth!

EXPLANATION

Once again we have used base and acid to create our old friend carbon dioxide. The citric acid reacts with the sodium bicarbonate to form sodium citrate and carbon dioxide and water. The sugar just makes it a bit more palatable.

$$C_6H_8O_7 + 3Na\,HCO_3 \rightarrow Na_3C_6H_5O_7. + 3CO_2 + 3H_2O$$

citric acid   +   sodium bicarbonate →   sodium citrate   +   carbon dioxide + water

SHERBET

This comes from the Arabic word *sharba*, meaning 'a drink'. In the nineteenth century sherbet powder was sold as a powder to be mixed with water to create a fizzy drink. It had to be drunk very quickly, or the re-action would take place so fast that the flavour would be lost. Thus it was marketed as sherbet fountains, in dynamite stick-like form.

Make Your Own Bath Bombs

I am sure that you have seen these fizzy balls that your sister or mum use in their baths. In contact with water they fizz and bubble and release a nice smell. Well, they are dead easy to make and they all depend on the same chemical reaction. Knowing how to make these may save you some money at birthday present buying time!

REQUIREMENTS

- ✓ a ping pong ball (table tennis ball) – cut a hole in the top and retain the cut out piece
- ✓ a larger Christmas bobble, of the type that consist of two hemispheres that snap together. This is ideal for the larger version
- ✓ citric acid powder
- ✓ sodium bicarbonate
- ✓ cornstarch
- ✓ glycerine solution

METHOD

I am going to give you the basic ingredients for the small ball. The proportion of the ingredients can be modified for larger ones.

Into a small bowl add two teaspoons of sodium bicarbonate, one teaspoon of starch and one teaspoon of citric acid. Add about 20 drops of glycerine (you may need to add more, but that is part of the experimenting). Mix it all up so that you have a crumbly powder. It mustn't be too moist, but it should be sticky enough to clump. If it won't clump, add more starch and glycerine.

Now pack your mould and keep tamping the mix down. Aim for a firm consistency, but don't make it too tight. Use the cut-out piece to smooth the ball into a good sphere. When you are ready, take the top off and gently cut down each side almost to the bottom of the ball with scissors, so that you can separate the two halves. You then remove the bath bomb and leave it somewhere warm for about an hour to dry.

You can reuse the mould. Just hold the two sides together as you pack it. Of course, the Christmas bobble may give you a better mould for the larger bath bombs, but that is the principle.

When it is dry drop it in a bath of water and watch it fizz.

Our old friend carbon dioxide has been formed by the reaction of base and acid. The glycerine does not react but helps to bind the bomb together.

Please note that I do not recommend adding oils or perfumes, since you never know if someone could react to such ingredients. If giving it as a gift, say that it is a scientifically manufactured bath bomb purely designed to demonstrate chemical effervescence! You may get brownie points from your grannie.

The phlogiston theory

The German chemist George Stahl (1660–1734) proposed a model in 1703 to explain what happens when substances are burned, or when metals like iron rust. He suggested that a substance he called **phlogiston** is released, which then leaves a residue, which he called a **calx**. The word phlogiston comes from the Greek *phlox*, meaning 'fire'. This would, of course, have fitted into the ancient Greek concept of the four elements. Accordingly, it was the dominant theory about combustion during the early eighteenth century.

As I mentioned above, Joseph Priestley, one of our greatest scientists, called his newly discovered gas 'dephlogisticated air'. He did this because the proper concept of a gas had not come into existence, there being only 'air' and 'fixed air' (carbon dioxide). Priestley himself was a firm supporter of the phlogiston theory and when he discovered the gas that we now call oxygen, he thought that it was air that had been dephlogisticated. He thought that this dephlogisticated air was capable of combining with more phlogiston from a burning substance, thereby allowing it to combust even more.

Although he went on to discover another ten further gases himself, including ammonia (NH_3), hydrogen chloride (HCl), nitrous oxide or laughing gas (N_2O) and sulphur dioxide (SO_2), it seems remarkable that he did not appreciate the naivety of phlogiston theory.

In 1776 Henry Cavendish[10] discovered hydrogen, which he called 'inflammable air' because it explodes when ignited. He did not realize that this was a gas, however, but thought that it was the mysterious substance 'phlogiston'.

It was left to the French scientist Antoine-Laurent de Lavoisier (1743–1794) to disprove the phlogiston theory once and for all. He demonstrated using completely closed vessels that combustion requires a gas – oxygen – in order for it to take place. There would be no alteration in the weight of the whole reaction, because phlogiston was not leaving the substance being combusted.

Sadly, since Lavoisier was also a tax collector, he fell victim to the

French Revolution and was sent to the guillotine at the age of 50. This was a tragic loss to science, since more than anyone else in disproving the phlogiston theory he had paved the way for the caloric theory of combustion.

Oxygen-Releasing Experiments

As you know, oxygen makes up 21 per cent of the air we breathe. It is manufactured industrially by the fractional distillation of liquefied air. That isn't easy to do in the home, so instead we shall use enzymatic reaction. Specifically, we shall use the enzyme **catalase**, found in living tissues. Two easily obtainable sources of it are liver from the butcher and yeast from the baker. You can also do this with macerated celery or other fruit and vegetables.

Do these experiments by the sink and only do them with your mum or dad's permission.

ENZYMES

Enzymes are substances present in living tissues that catalyze (help) all sorts of chemical reactions in the living cells.

1 Yeast Catalase

REQUIREMENTS

- ✓ hydrogen peroxide (H_2O_2), obtainable from the chemist. Careful with this, it can bleach surfaces if spilled. It is used as an antiseptic. Always wash it off your hands
- ✓ small glass jar
- ✓ dried yeast – ¼ teaspoon
- ✓ a large glass dish or bowl
- ✓ postcard
- ✓ 2 small lids, which will balance the upturned jar in the dish. If you can't get small ones then use coins instead

METHOD

Place the lids in the bottom of the dish and then pour hydrogen peroxide into the dish, so that you cover the lids by about a centimetre. Half fill the jar with hydrogen peroxide and add the dried yeast. Stir the yeast round and then place the postcard over the jar mouth. Turn it over and lower it into the dish, aiming to balance it on the lids. Slide the postcard out and the experiment is set.

You will find that it bubbles slowly. Let this go on for about two hours. You will find that a gas has pushed all of the liquid out of the jar. Upend it and immediately cover with the postcard. This gas is oxygen, and you can test it with a glowing taper. That is a taper that has been lit then blown out. If you remove the card and put the glowing taper in the jar it will pop and burst into flame.

THE TEST FOR OXYGEN

Oxygen is colourless and has no smell. It does not react with litmus or universal indicator. It reignites a glowing splint or taper.

2 Liver Catalase

The yeast enzyme is quite a gentle process. Liver catalase is remarkably fast.

REQUIREMENTS

✓ a small piece of liver – about an inch square is all
✓ hydrogen peroxide
✓ a small jar

METHOD

Place the liver in the jar and pour on enough hydrogen peroxide to cover it by a centimetre. The reaction will be instantaneous and the liquid will effervesce, giving off bubbles of oxygen.

A glowing splint will immediately pop and reignite, since this is so fast.

Liver Catalase experiment

The catalase in both of these experiments decomposes hydrogen peroxide into water and oxygen:

$$2H_2O_2 \quad \rightarrow \quad 2H_2O \quad + \quad O_2$$

This is actually an extremely important reaction in living cells. Hydrogen peroxide is produced as a toxic by-product in respiration. All living cells will produce some of it. All organisms that obtain their energy from the oxidation of food have had to develop a means of getting rid of it, since it damages cells.

We looked at yeast in the chapter on Cooking Chemistry. You will recall that it is able to operate both in the presence of or in the absence of oxygen. When oxygen is absent (**anaerobic** conditions) it causes fermentation of sugars to produce alcohol and carbon dioxide. In the presence of oxygen (**aerobic** conditions) it undergoes respiration to produce carbon dioxide and water.

But, in fact, when it respires it will also produce small quantities of hydrogen peroxide as well. And that is where the yeast's catalase comes into action. It gets rid of this hydrogen peroxide by decomposing it into water and oxygen, which are both helpful to it.

You can repeat these experiments with any fruit or vegetable. Just cut it up or macerate it and pour hydrogen peroxide over it. Small bubbles of oxygen will start to form. Indeed, when hydrogen peroxide is used as an antiseptic, it may be applied to a cut. It will effervesce, because the catalase in the cut tissues will decompose it into oxygen and water.

The Soda Geyser experiment

But you will not see any of these other experiments effervesce as well as with the liver.

The Great Soda Geyser Experiment

This really is a spectacular experiment to do outside. And one to be careful about. Don't get too near it or you will get a sticky soaking!

✓ 1 large 2-litre plastic bottle of cola or potentially fizzy drink
✓ a pack of fizzy mint sweets

METHOD

Place the bottle outside on a lawn, well propped up so that it cannot tumble over. Place about four of the mints (and they should be the type that will fizz, not smooth coated ones) on the rim of the bottle and tip them in – then run for it.

The result is a soda geyser.

EXPLANATION

There has been controversy about this experiment. It certainly is a great fizz experiment, for you produce carbon dioxide bubbles in abundance, which will shoot out as foam for 10, 12, 15 feet. You can experiment with different types of mints – and many will not work. It seems that the mints have lots of little cavities that allow bubbles to form very rapidly to produce foam. Thus it is partly a chemical and partly a physical reaction.

Either way it is spectacular.

CHAPTER SEVEN

THE GENIUS OF SIR ISAAC NEWTON

Isaac Newton (1642–1727) was born at Woolsthorpe Manor in the county of Lincolnshire on Christmas Day 1642. A sickly child, he was to become one of the foremost scientific geniuses of all time.

He was educated at the local school, from where he went to Cambridge University in 1661 and graduated in 1665. His genius was apparent to all and he was elected a Fellow of Trinity College in 1667 before becoming the Lucasian Professor of Mathematics in 1669, at the age of 27. In 1671 he was elected a Fellow of the Royal Society and in 1703 became the president, a post he held until his death.

He stayed and lectured in Cambridge until 1696 when he moved to London to become the Warden of the Royal Mint. Three years later he became Master of the Mint. In 1705 he was knighted.

That is quite a remarkable string of achievements, yet they give only the bare outline of the man. As you will find out in this book his name is dotted all over the field of science. He made countless discoveries, conducted innumerable meticulous experiments across the fields of optics, fluid dynamics, mechanics and astronomy, and even invented a whole new branch of mathematics, which we now know as calculus.[11] It seems only fitting to give him a little space to himself in this book.

Sir Isaac Newton – courtesy of The Whipple Museum, University of Cambridge

THE FAMOUS FALLING APPLE

Every schoolboy and schoolgirl must surely have heard about the apple that Isaac Newton saw fall (some versions of the tale say it fell on his head), which set him thinking about the force that made it fall. We can in fact date this to either 1665 or 1666, because plague had broken out in London and fears of its spread were rife. Cambridge University was closed down to limit spread of the disease. Newton returned to Woolsthorpe Manor and studied and thought on his own during this time. He described seeing the apple drop from a tree in the manor garden. And if you are interested, the tree is still there.

This was the germ of an idea that he developed into his gravitational theory, which he published in his famous three volumes, *Philosophia Naturalis Mathematica Principia* (*Mathematical Principles of Natural Philosophy*), in 1687. It is usually just referred to as *Principia*.

OPTICS AND NEWTON'S RINGS

While he was a student he studied the work of Robert Boyle and Robert Hooke on optics, as well as the mathematics and theories of René Descartes. He then built on this and with meticulous experimentation with prisms and light he made significant discoveries about colour and the nature of white light. He found that it was in fact made up of several different-coloured rays, and that it could be split into the spectrum or rainbow pattern that happens naturally when it rains. He came to believe that light was made up of a continuous flow of minute particles that he called 'corpuscles'. He described all this in his major work, *Opticks*, published in 1704.

His work on optics and astronomy led him to study lenses. He noted a phenomenon of chromatic aberration, in which certain lens combinations could produce a splitting of the light to produce blurring of the image and the production of concentric rings that could interfere with the image. When this is viewed with monochromatic light, or light of one colour, it produces concentric dark rings, but with white light it produces rings of the rainbow. In order to avoid this effect while studying the heavens he invented the reflecting telescope.

MATHEMATICS AND CALCULUS

As the Lucasian Professor of Mathematics he made major contributions to many branches of mathematics. As mentioned above, he is known to have invented calculus, without which it would be impossible to make much headway in mathematics and physics. This is a means by which one can compare quantities that vary in a non-linear way. It has two branches – **differentiation**, which is used to find a rate of change of one quantity compared to another; and **integration**, or the reverse process, when we need to work backwards to find the relationship or relevant equation between the two quantities.

MECHANICS, GRAVITY AND THE THREE LAWS OF MOTION

In his three-volume work Newton effectively lays down the basis of physics. The first book is about mechanics and introduces the concept of a force of gravity. Book two is about fluids and the movement of fluids. In this book he calculated the speed of sound. Book three gives his theory of universal gravitation.

Newton proposed three laws concerning the relationship between force, motion, acceleration, mass and inertia.

Newton's first law, or the law of inertia: a body at rest will remain at rest, and a body in motion will remain in motion with a constant velocity, unless acted upon by a force.

Newton's second law: a force acting on a body is equal to the acceleration of that body times its mass.

Thus: $F = ma$ where F is the force in Newtons, m is the mass of the body in kilograms, and a the acceleration in metres per second per second.

Newton's Cradle

Newton's third law: for every action there is an equal and opposite reaction. Thus, if one body exerts a force **F** on a second body, the first body also undergoes a force of the same strength but in the opposite direction.

The 'executive toy' known as Newton's cradle is useful for demonstrating these three laws. It was named in honour of Newton.

A FLAWED GENIUS

While one has to acknowledge Newton's genius, it also has to be mentioned that he was an irascible fellow. He disliked any personal criticism or suggestion that he had not made the discoveries he claimed. When Robert Hooke wrote to him, having felt aggrieved that his work had not been suitably acknowledged, Newton systematically removed any reference to him in his future books. And his dispute with Liebniz over calculus went on for many years. Newton even published a report under the auspices of the Royal Society accusing Leibniz of plagiarism. Sadly, the dispute did not even end when Leibniz died. This had the effect of the Newtonian theories being badly received on the Continent for the better part of a century.

Newton was equally vindictive and assiduous in his role as Warden of the Mint. He orchestrated a campaign against counterfeiting, and was instrumental in having several men executed.

CHAPTER EIGHT

CRYSTALS

I am sure that you will have made crystals at school. Prang, my old chemistry teacher, was very proud of his collection of crystals that he had grown and preserved over the years. He kept them under lock and key and brought them out to show successive generations of kids when he came to teach them about the wonders of crystallization. He kept each specimen in a little pill box, wrapped up in cotton wool. They were produced with great panache, drawing our attention to their facets, the perfection of their faces and the purity of their colour. You would have thought that they were precious jewels from lands afar instead of simple chemicals.

Yet as he taught us about them and set us several experiments to do, we were all hooked. Then he capitalized on that enthusiasm and started a competition to see who could grow the best copper sulphate crystal. The prize was a giant bar of chocolate, a great incentive in those days.

There is a staggering range of natural crystals

91

Sadly, I did not win! I suspect to this very day that it was because my solution had been sabotaged. I had friends who were capable of such things. Yet no matter, I enjoyed the experiments and the knowledge of how to make crystals fired me with enthusiasm to see if I could make some of my own at home, using ordinary household products. And writing this book stimulated me to repeat those experiments.

CRYSTALLIZATION

A crystal is a solid composed of atoms or molecules arranged in a specific pattern in all three dimensions. The study of crystals is called **crystallography**. We are going to use the process of **crystallization** to grow our crystals.

Firstly, you need to make a **saturated solution** of the substance you want to crystallize. This means that the **solvent** cannot dissolve any more of the **solute** in it.

Nucleation is the name of the process that occurs as crystals start to form. In **unassisted nucleation** some solute molecules will aggregate to form a proto-crystal, which you will not see, because it is so small and it is floating about in the solution. Eventually other solute molecules will join it and locate in a set manner and a crystal will start to fall out of solution.

In **assisted nucleation** some solid surface acts as a focus point upon which a crystal will start to form. If you want to grow a crystal garden, then a rock, stone or sponge will do this job.

Once crystals have started to fall out of solution, they will continue to do so until equilibrium has been reached between the molecules in the crystal and the solution. So, if you are growing crystals you have to ensure that the solution remains saturated.

HOW TO GROW CRYSTALS

Firstly, make a saturated solution of the substance you want to crystallize. This can be a sugar, salt or baking ingredient. Most will dissolve better in hot or boiled water. Just keep adding solute until no more will dissolve. If you end up with a sediment, then filter the solution through a coffee filter into a glass beaker.

You can easily make a crystal garden by pouring the solution over a rock or a sponge and just letting it evaporate. If you want to grow a single large crystal then you need to get a seed crystal, so just pour a little of the saturated solution on to a plate and let it evaporate to produce some crystals. Select the most uniform one that you can and gently tie nylon fishing line

Alum cyrstals are easy to grow

or the finest thread around it and tie the end to a pencil. Then suspend this in the saturated solution and place a tissue paper over the surface. Then just leave it and keep watching. If crystals form on the string, remove them, and if crystals form in the beaker, get rid of them and pour your solution (keeping it saturated) into a clean beaker and then resuspend your growing crystal in it.

This is important, since other crystals will compete with your growing one for further solute. If there are a lot of other crystals then they can affect the equilibrium point when no further crystallization will take place.

I would recommend that you try making crystals from what you'll find in the kitchen – household salt, white sugar, brown sugar, baking powder, tartaric acid, bicarbonate of soda. From the bathroom, try Epsom salts (magnesium sulphate), and from the laundry room, washing soda (hydrated sodium carbonate). You can, if you wish, taint solutions with food colouring, or you can be a true chemist like old Prang and try to grow pure crystals.

Once made, the crystals will need to be kept dry and away from humid conditions, or they will start to dissolve. Wrap them in cotton wool or tissue and keep them separate from each other in little boxes. Assuming that you want to keep them at all, that is.

And you can reward yourself with a giant chocolate bar. I did!

STALACTITES AND STALAGMITES

These always fascinated me. No adventure film about caves or travelling to the centre of the earth would be complete without some majestic stalactites or stalagmites. Prang taught us that the way to remember which is which is that the stalactites are 'tite' to the roof.

They are formed by water containing carbon dioxide seeping through limestone (calcium carbonate) to produce calcium bicarbonate solution. Thus:

$$CaCO_{3\ [solid]} + H_2O_{[liquid]} + CO_{2[in\ solution]} \rightarrow Ca(HCO_3)_{2\ [in\ solution]}$$

calcium carbonate + water + carbon dioxide → calcium bicarbonate

When this reaches an opening, i.e. the roof of a cave, it will contact with air again and the chemical reaction will be reversed and calcium carbonate will be deposited. Thus:

$$Ca(HCO_3)_{2\ [in\ solution]} \rightarrow CaCO_{3\ [solid]} + H_2O_{[liquid]} + CO_{2\ [in\ solution]}$$

calcium bicarbonate → calcium carbonate + water + carbon dioxide

These amazing structures found in limestone caves around the world are good measurements of time. The average growth rate of a stalactite is 0.13 millimetres or 0.005 inches per year. A fast-growing one under a fast flowing river under the right chemical conditions can grow at 3 millimetres or 0.12 inches a year. When you see huge ones, they put time into perspective.

Now, I am sure you will have seen stalactite formations under bridges or in old cellars. Clearly these did not take so long to form as the ones in caves. The reason is that they are chemically different. They are formed from the calcium oxide in concrete, but the process is the same. The chemical reaction here is for the carbon dioxide in the water seeping through to react with the calcium oxide to form calcium hydroxide. Thus:

$$CaO_{[solid]} + H_2O_{[liquid]} \rightarrow Ca(OH)_{2\ [in\ solution]}$$

calcium oxide + water → calcium hydroxide

When this seeps through to a roof or ceiling surface the calcium hydroxide will react with carbon dioxide in the air to form calcium carbonate, which will be deposited to form a mini stalactite. Thus:

$$Ca(OH)_{2\ [in\ solution]} + CO2_{[air]} \rightarrow CaCO_{3\ [solid]} + H_2O_{[liquid]}$$

calcium hydroxide + carbon dioxide → calcium carbonate + water

The Stalactite And Stalagmite Experiment

Don't worry, you don't need to go near any caves to do this. You are going to make your own stalactites and stalagmites – with bicarbonate of soda.

REQUIREMENTS

✓ 2 beakers
✓ length of wool
✓ a couple of weights (2 stones will do)
✓ a tray
✓ saturated solution of sodium bicarbonate

METHOD

Make a saturated solution of sodium bicarbonate (baking soda). Pour it equally into the two beakers. Take the length of wool and tie a stone on each end. Soak the wool in the solution, then arrange it on the tray so that you have one stone in each beaker and the wool draped between the beakers, slightly hanging down.

Just wait and watch. After two or three days you will find that crystals start to form on the wool. These are stalactites. Just leave them longer and longer, just making sure that you keep topping up the saturated solutions in the beakers and avoiding crystal build up within them, or they will affect the equilibrium. Eventually, if you wait long enough, you may get stalagmites forming underneath the stalactites.

And if you do, I know that Prang would have been proud of you.

CHAPTER NINE

FLOPPY VEG AND CRISPY FRUIT

OK, so what is the difference between a fruit and a vegetable?

That may sound a silly question, but it depends who you are talking to: a greengrocer or a scientist. A greengrocer would say that fruits have seeds and vegetables don't. A scientist would tell you that a fruit is the ripened ovary or seedbox of a flower. Actually, a vegetable is not a scientific term at all. Instead the scientist would talk about the plant or the parts of a plant. Thus, lettuce (leaves), potato (root tubers), carrots (tap roots), onion (bulbs) would all be considered vegetables by a greengrocer and plant parts by a scientist.

Similarly, apples, pears, oranges and bananas are all considered fruits by a scientist. Yet so too are tomatoes, peppers and marrows, whereas a greengrocer would consider them to be vegetables! Strawberries are 'false fruits' since they actually have their seeds on the outside. Have a look next time you have a strawberry.

So, if you want to be correct about all this, think of fruits as being ripened seedboxes, so that if you cut through them you will find seeds. You won't find them in vegetables, unless they are false vegetables (i.e. real fruits) like marrows, squashes, peppers, chillies and tomatoes. And the biggest of them all, the pumpkin, is a fruit.

Cucumber: a really cool vegetable. I mean fruit

This is an easy one to test. Just slice one and there are the seeds in the middle. You know the old expression, as 'cool as a cucumber'? Do you want to know where that came from?

Cucumbers have been cultivated for at least 3,000 years. They originated in the foothills of the Himalayas, in modern-day India. Like other precious commodities they found their way to Egypt thence to the Mediterranean. The Romans used them for all manner of things, including medicine.

Cucumber was one of the Galenical medicines. That is, it was included in prescriptions made up by Galen, a famous second-century physician, because it was a 'cooling fruit'. In antiquity doctors practised medicine according to the Doctrine of Signatures. This was a belief that nature had given clues about the healing ability of various plants and minerals, what they referred to as their 'signatures'. Cucumber was known to grow in hot conditions, yet when cut open it was always cool inside (try it yourself and see). Thus it was used to cool temperatures and when rubbed on parts of the body it would cool and reduce inflammation. Modern science reveals that it is rich in salicylates (aspirin, one of our best painkillers and temperature reducers, is acetyl-salicyclic acid).

IS YOUR BATH SPONGE ANIMAL, VEGETABLE OR SYNTHETIC?

Early Europeans used sponges to clean all sorts of things. They are actually tiny aquatic animals that grow in colonies. Their calcium is generally too hard and scratchy for use on the body, but two genera of them are softer. Synthetic sponges are generally to be found in the bathroom, the kitchen or as padding for clothes, sportswear and so on.

The loofah in the bathroom is often mistakenly called a sponge. It is not an animal at all, but a fibrous gourd, related to the cucumber. Just look at the shape of it and you will see that it is a great big seedbox.

PLANT CELLS

Robert Hooke (1635–1703), who we shall meet again in the chapter Down the Microscope, first coined the term 'cell' in 1665, from the Latin *cella*, meaning small room. He was examining sections of cork with an early microscope and described the pores that he saw as units of life. In actual fact it was not until the nineteenth century that the units that we now accept as cells were discovered, yet in honour of his achievements, his term for the cell was kept.

Plant cells are quite different from animal cells, although they do have some common features, suggestive of a common distant ancestry.

The living part of the cell is called the **protoplasm**. This has two parts. The **nucleus** is the controller of the

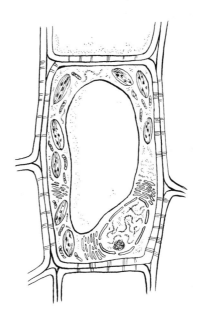

A typical plant cell

cell and the storage space of all the genetic material, contained in the inherited chromosomes of the cell. This was first described by the botanist Robert Brown in 1831. Secondly, the **cytoplasm** is jelly-like fluid in which most of the cell's metabolic processes and reactions take place. The cytoplasm is contained within the **cytoplasmic membrane**, which is made of protein and fatty acids. It allows the movement of water, nutrients and minerals in and out of the cell. It is a semi-permeable membrane, which thereby allows the very important process of **osmosis** to take place. We shall return to this shortly.

There are various structures collectively termed **organelles** floating within the cytoplasm. One type of organelle, the **chloroplast**, is unique to plant cells. It contains the green pigment **chlorophyll**, which is essential to the process of **photosynthesis**, which allows plants to use light energy to build food.

Mitochondria are small organelles that permit the process of **cellular respiration** to take place (which we discussed in Chapter Two on Cooking Chemistry). **Ribosomes** are another highly important type of organelle involved in protein reproduction. They are scattered about the cytoplasm like little dots.

The **vacuole** is a large bubble of fluid in the centre of the cell filled with water, essential minerals and also waste products of the cell's metabolism.

Surrounding the cytoplasmic membrane is the **cell wall**, a relatively rigid structure made of cellulose. This is protective of the cell. These are only found in plant cells. The individual cell walls are bound together by the **middle lamella**, which is made of a substance called **pectin**, which is used to make jelly and jam.

PHOTOSYNTHESIS

This is the process by which plants and some bacteria use the energy of light to convert carbon dioxide and water into sugar and oxygen. The sugar is converted in the cells into usable energy, which fuels the metabolic processes of life. The oxygen is released into the atmosphere, and is breathed in by animals, including humans. This reaction takes place in the chloroplasts, in the presence of the all-important chlorophyll:

$$6H_2O + 6CO_2 \rightarrow C_6H_{12}O_6 + 6O_2$$
$$\text{Water} + \text{Carbon dioxide} \rightarrow \text{Glucose} + \text{Oxygen}$$

A Simple Photosynthesis Experiment
The technique for testing photosynthesis is very simple and easily done – with care – in the kitchen laboratory.

✓ a growing plant – a geranium is easy to work with
✓ a test tube containing a little alcohol
✓ a beaker or pan
✓ aluminium foil
✓ tincture of iodine

METHOD

Place the plant in the dark for 24 hours. This will ensure that starch is moved by the plant from the leaves. Then cover one part of a leaf with silver foil – you can make a pattern if you want to be smart. Now expose the plant to sunlight for a day. After 24 hours remove the foil and cut off the leaf. Drop it into a beaker or a pan of boiling water for one minute to soften the leaf. Then take it and drop it into the test tube containing the alcohol (enough so that it is immersed) and carefully place this into the pan or beaker, keeping it upright. This will leach all of the green from the leaf. Once all of the green has come out, remove the leaf and dab dry on kitchen roll.

Place it in a saucer and drop iodine on to it. You will find that the blanched leaf will turn brown where the leaf was covered and it will go inky blue wherever it had been exposed to light.

EXPLANATION

Iodine is the test for starch. It goes blue in the presence of starch. Photosynthesis will only take place in the light, so only in the light exposed parts of the leaf will starch have been produced.

OSMOSIS

This is the process whereby water diffuses across a semi-permeable membrane from an area of low-solute concentration to one of high-solute concentration. It is the water pump of the cell.

Water is absorbed into the roots of a plant by this process. Effectively, during osmosis water molecules attempt to equalize the concentrations on the two sides of the semi-permeable membrane (it only lets certain things like water through).

When plants have plenty of water they are nice and crisp and when they lack fluid they go floppy.

The Floppy Brown Potato Experiment
See a potato shrivel and brown when you salt it.

REQUIREMENTS

✓ a large potato
✓ a knife
✓ a plate
✓ 1 teaspoon
✓ ¼ teaspoon of salt
✓ (dishwasher!)

METHOD

Select a large potato and carefully cut it in half. Place both halves of the potato on a plate, cut side down. Now with a teaspoon scoop out a hole in the top of each potato piece. Each hole should be big enough to stick the tip of your thumb into and deep enough to take the length of the nail. Leave one just as it is, but drop about a quarter of a teaspoon of salt into the other. Leave the plate and check it in about 15 minutes.

WHAT HAPPENS?

When you come back you will find that the unsalted potato looks just the same, but the salted one will have water in the salt. And the surrounding potato will probably have turned a bit brown. Leave it for a couple of hours and the difference will be quite striking. The salted potato will have started to go floppy and after a few hours will shrivel, go yucky brown and grey–brown goo will accumulate on the plate. On the other hand, the plain one will have just started to go brown.

EXPLANATION

This is a good and very simple example of the process of osmosis. This is one of the driving forces of the cells in all living things. The salt you placed

The Floppy
Brown Potato
experiment

inside the hole in the potato dissolved in the small amount of juice that was released when you cut the hole. This made a very concentrated salt solution, which pulled more water from the cells. The water pulled from the cells dissolved more salt, letting the salt solution reach more cells, to take more water from the potato.

OXIDATIVE BROWNING

The browning of the potato is also interesting. It occurs because of damage to the cells themselves. Pulling all that water from inside them damaged them and caused them to release an enzyme called **catechol oxidase**. This combines with oxygen in the air to produce the brown colour. Technically, it catalyzes the conversion of phenolic compounds in the potato tissue to melanins.[12] Eventually, the plain potato will turn brown as well, since some of its cells were damaged from the cutting, but the salt causes much more cell damage and more browning.

This browning effect happens with many other fruits and vegetables. As you probably know, bananas react quickest of all. You may think that this is because they are going bad, but actually that is not the case. It does create a headache for food producers and fruit sellers, since the idea of browning is so fixed in the public's mind as indicating that the fruit is past its best.

Apple Browning Experiment
See if you can deduce what factors affect enzymatic browning.

REQUIREMENTS

✓ an apple
✓ 1 clean knife
✓ 1 rusty knife
✓ saucers containing white vinegar, lemon juice, citric acid, water

METHOD

Cut an apple into pieces and remove the core from them all. Drop a piece into the saucers containing white vinegar, lemon juice, citric acid and water and leave one exposed to the air. You might also see if there is a difference when you cut the apple with a clean knife or with a rusty knife.

Leave them for half an hour, assessing them and scoring them every 10 minutes. Use this rating from 1 to 5:

1	=	no browning
2	=	slight patchy browning
3	=	half covered light brown
4	=	all coloured light brown
5	=	all over dark brown

I will leave you to find out what results you get, but I expect that you will get a gradation of effects rather like this. The control exposed to air will probably brown quickest. Then the one in water, then the vinegar and citric acid, then the lemon juice.

A lot depend on the pH of the acids you use. Browning takes place mainly in the pH range 5–7, so if your acids are stronger than 5, i.e. 3–5, then they will inhibit the enzyme. Lemon juice contains ascorbic acid and citric acid, so the ascorbic acid inhibits the oxidation itself.

The apple cut with the rusty knife will brown quicker, except in the citric acid. This is because the presence of iron enhances the oxidation. Citric acid inactivates this mechanism.

You may have noticed that your mum puts a little lemon juice into her fruit salad to stop it going brown – well, now you know why.

TRANSLOCATION

This is the process by which a plant moves water, food and nutrients about within it. That is, it moves starch and sugars down from the leaves to its food stores (which may be the roots, the stem or a variant) and moves water from the roots to the tips of every part of the plant.

There are two types of conducting tissue in plants, the **xylem** and the **phloem**. They extend as tubes from the tips of the roots to the tips of the leaves. The xylem tissue dies off and remains as rigid hollow tubes of very small diameter. Their function is to transmit water up the plant from the roots. The phloem are living tissue and transmit food down from the leaves to their storage in the roots.

Marcelo Malpighi (1628–1694) discovered this conducting system by an experiment in 1697. He found that if a ring of bark was removed from a tree then eventually the bark below the cutting would shrivel and dry up, whereas the bark above would swell and bulge as if it was accumulating some fluid. His conclusion was that some channels that ran down had been cut away. He also noted that if the leaves were off the tree, this effect did not occur. He conjectured that the leaves produced food and that it was the food channels that were cut away when the bark ring was removed.

And so let us see if we can demonstrate part of this process.

The Xylem Experiment
We do not propose to damage any trees, merely use a couple of sticks of celery.

✓ 2 sticks of celery, 1 with the leaves intact and 1 with the leaves chopped off
✓ red food colouring in solution

METHOD

Cut the bottom off each celery stick and place them in a jar containing the food dye. Depending upon how impatient you are, you can have a look after as little as half an hour to see an effect, or wait a whole day and you will see the whole process.

If you peel back the outer skin you will see that the dye has moved up tiny tubes. Look at the ends and you will see where the tubes start. The main mechanism is capillary action, but in the case of the stick with leaves, the dye will eventually move all the way up to the very tips of the leaves. This is partly because the leaves will help to suck the water up.

And as *Monty Python* would say, now for something completely different.

A Ghostly Experiment For Halloween

Halloween is a great time to try out this experiment. It is of course the night when ghosts, ghouls and spirits are supposed to come knocking on your door. That is why it is traditional to carve a pumpkin lantern. While you are about it this year, you might care to try this little experiment to see if you can raise the spirit of the pumpkin!

REQUIREMENTS

✓ 1 pumpkin
✓ 20 millilitres of plain, chilled alcohol (your dad's gin or vodka) or even surgical spirit, since this is purely for experimental purposes, definitely **not** for drinking. Put this in the fridge for at least an hour (preferably two) before you begin.

METHOD

As you carve the pumpkin, chop up about a cupful of the pumpkin flesh and pop it into a food blender, along with a dessert spoonful of salt. Add about a dessert spoonful of water and start it off. You are aiming to reduce this mix to the consistency of apple sauce. You may need to add a little more water to do so. Then add a couple of dessert spoonfuls of washing-up liquid, preferably the clear type, but it doesn't matter if you only have green detergent. Give it another buzz round, which will produce a foam.

Now, pass this foamy puree through a coffee filter paper. If you haven't got one just make a cone out of kitchen roll. Let this clear fluid drip into a test tube. You need to be able to see the liquid clearly. Next get the

The spirit of the pumpkin

alcohol out of the fridge and tilt the test tube containing the filtered detergent very slightly. Then very, very carefully pour the alcohol down the side of the glass so that it forms a layer on top of the oily fluid. And then watch carefully.

After a few seconds a ghostly layer will start to form between the juice and the alcohol. It will be like the white ectoplasm that you see in ghost films. And it is literally the spirit of the pumpkin!

EXPLANATION

And what do I mean by the spirit of the pumpkin? Well, believe it or not, you will have just extracted the DNA from the pumpkin flesh. And the DNA is literally the spirit, the very essence, of this particular pumpkin.

The pumpkin flesh is made up of water, cellulose, sugar, protein, salts and DNA. The blender literally broke down all the cellulose fibres that were holding the plant cells together, so that they all separated. This allowed the salt and the detergent to get to the cell walls, where they attached themselves to the fatty acids in the cell membranes and caused them to burst open. As a result, the DNA from inside the cells leaked out into the fluid and dissolved in the water. When you added the alcohol, it precipitated the DNA out of the water as the white ghost. Spooky!

DNA

You may be tempted to look at the DNA that you have extracted under your microscope, but I am afraid that you will not see very much except some proteinaceaus clumping. But now that you have extracted some of this amazing stuff, let's talk about it.

In 1953 James D Watson and Francis Crick elucidated the structure of **DNA** or **deoxyribose nucleic acid**. They won the 1962 Nobel Prize for Medicine for their work on nucleic acids.

DNA is the double helix protein molecule that contains the genetic information about a person. It is a blueprint or code about the individual. Genes are made up of sequences of DNA, which are joined in long strands called **chromosomes**. Each cell has about 20,000 to 25,000 genes located on 23 pairs of chromosomes. One of these chromosome pairs consist of sex chromosomes, which determine what sex the individual will be. The genes determine all of the individual's potential traits. They can be switched on or off in certain circumstances.

Some More Fruit And Veg Experiments

I am going to return to the amazing electrical properties of fruit in a later chapter on Magnetism and Electricity, to which you might like to short circuit right now! Otherwise, let us look at some of the interesting things in the fruit bowl and the vegetable basket.

The Unzip A Banana Experiment

This is similar to the Egg in a Bottle experiment described in Chapter Four.

REQUIREMENTS

✓ 1 banana
✓ 1 empty plastic bottle or a milk bottle
✓ 3 matches

METHOD

Just open the end of the banana and light the three matches and drop them into the bottle, letting them burn. Then straight away place the banana over the mouth of the bottle. As the flames go out, the banana will peel itself into the bottle.

It is quite impressive, but it will not be pleasant to eat!

Essential Peel Experiment

Make some spectacular flashes when you peel citrus fruits.

✓ a candle
✓ orange, lemon or lime peel

METHOD
Light the candle and holding the peel a couple of inches away from the flame squeeze hard to spray some peel juice at the flame. You will produce a spectacular coloured flame. See if there is a different colour with the different fruits.

EXPLANATION
The peel of the citrus fruits contains essential oils. These are all used commercially.

The Onion v Potato Race Experiment
You need a potato that has started to sprout and an onion that has also started to sprout. You are going to see if they can grow their way out of a maze – and which is fastest! You also need to construct a maze out of a couple of shoe boxes.

METHOD
Just cut the second shoe box up and insert dividing sections in the first one, making, say, three sections. Cut holes so that there is an erratic way out. Now place your onion and the potato together at opposite ends of one section. Make sure that there is a hole in the box at the end, through which light can get into the box. Now close the box and leave it for about two or three weeks and then check on what is happening.

You will find that the sprouts find a way through the maze towards the light. Any bets on which will win?

EXPLANATION
This is all to do with plant hormones. Have you ever wondered how seeds know how to send shoots upwards and roots downwards? Well they do this by producing hormones with differing actions.

Phototropism is the effect of causing a part to grow towards the light. That is what is happening here. **Autotropism** is the tendency to grow straight. **Gravitropism** is the process whereby roots grow down and shoots grow up.

The popcorn effect

Do you like popcorn? I do and can never resist buying a bag when I go to the movies. Interestingly, popcorn has been around for a long time.

Apparently, archaeologists have found fragments of cooked popcorn in a New Mexico cave that have been carbon dated and found to be 4,000 years old.

A corn kernel has three main parts, consisting of the pericarp or husk, the starchy endosperm on the inside and the germ, which becomes the corn plant. When you heat the corn kernel the pericarp holds in the steam created when the endosperm, which is made up of 14.5 per cent water, heats up. This happens incredibly quickly, the internal temperature rising to 350° and 135 pounds per square inch. The pericarp then pops and the starch explodes. It effectively turns itself inside out. This is the popcorn effect. Those yellow stringy bits that get stuck between teeth are the remnants of the percarp, which have been blown inside out.

The strange case of asparagus

If you have ever eaten asparagus at a meal it is almost inevitable that someone will bring up the subject of the effect asparagus has on the urine. If you are not aware of this, it makes the urine smell strange – rather like rotten or boiled cabbage. But the thing is that only about 50 per cent of people notice this effect. It really is an intriguing little mystery.

In fact, it has been known about for a long time. An eighteenth-century physician to the French royal family wrote a treatise about various types of food, and commented that when asparagus is eaten to excess it 'causes a filthy and disagreeable smell in the urine'.

Asparagus belongs to the lily family, along with garlic, onions and leeks. It was first cultivated about 2,500 years ago in Greece, and the name comes from the Greek word meaning stalk or shoot. The Greeks believed that it had important medicinal qualities, and that it was of value in toothache and that it stopped bees and insects from stinging.

Asparagus contains a substance called **mercaptan** (also present in rotten eggs, onions and garlic), which is broken down by the digestive tract into a number of sulphur-containing by-products. The main one, **methyl mercaptan**, is responsible for the smell. It will be passed in the urine 15 to 30 minutes after eating a couple of asparagus stalks.

There have been several research studies done on this curious phenomenon. Most trials have found that about 50 per cent of people can smell this boiled cabbage odour in their urine, and 50 per cent cannot. This caused debate among scientists as to whether it was due to the presence or absence of a particular enzyme that breaks down mercaptan.

But another research trial found that when the urine of everyone in a study was analyzed, it seemed that most people did actually produce the substance methyl mercaptan, but that only 50 per cent could smell it. Interestingly, those who could smell it in their own urine could also smell it in the urine samples of other people, even in those who could not smell it themselves. Thus, the mystery has been solved. There is a genetic inheritable pattern, but it is the ability to detect the smell of methyl mercaptan that is actually genetically determined.

Asparagus is good for you. It is one of the richest sources of folic acid, potassium, thiamine, vitamins A, C and B6. I heartily recommend it as a vegetable.

AN EMBARRASSING EXPERIMENT – IF YOU DARE!

I am sure you can guess what I mean. If 50 per cent can smell it and 50 per cent can't, get a group of asparagus-eating people all to go to the loo and ask each to pass a small specimen of urine in a specimen container. Ask them if they can smell anything odd about their urine. Divide the group into those who can smell something odd and those who cannot. Then get everyone to swap their sample with someone in the other group. Those who couldn't smell it in their own will not be able to smell it in the urine of those who did smell it. Those who smelled it in their own should also be able to smell it in the urine of those who can't.

That is what should happen. Try the experiment – as I said, if you dare!

CHAPTER TEN

EUREKA!

There is no finer image in the history of science than that of Archimedes of Syracuse (c287–210BC) dashing naked from his bath after solving a problem. It is worth a little retelling since it is a suitable introduction to this chapter devoted to the bathroom and liquids in general.

King Hieron of Syracuse had a crown made by a jeweller from a block of gold, yet although the crown weighed the same as the block he was suspicious as to whether the jeweller had used all of the gold, or whether he had substituted some silver. He handed the problem to Archimedes, who was initially unable to come up with an answer, until one day he got into his bath and the solution presented itself to him.

So ecstatic was he upon arriving at a possible solution that he immediately rose from his bath and ran naked down the streets crying 'Eureka!' ('I have found it!')

Eureka!

ARCHIMEDES' PRINCIPLE

Archimedes had discovered an important principle that has been formulated into the famous Archimedes' Principle. This is: any object, wholly or partially immersed in a fluid, is buoyed up by a force equal to the weight of the fluid displaced by the object.

So, by immersing the crown in a bath of water and collecting the water that would be displaced by it, he could determine the volume of the crown. By then dividing the weight of the crown by the volume of water that had been displaced the density of the crown could be calculated. This density would be lower than that of gold if a cheaper metal had been added.

Archimedes deserved his reward. It is uncertain what fate befell the jeweller!

SURFACE TENSION

The surface tension of a liquid or fluid is the property that makes it behave like an elastic sheet. Thus the surface tension of water allows insects like the pond-skater to skip across its surface, small metal objects to float, and helps fluid rise in fine tubes as the capillary action we talked about in the last chapter when we considered the xylem tubes of plants.

This comes about because of the attraction of like molecules through the forces of cohesion. Thus, a molecule within the middle of a mass of liquid experiences **cohesive forces** from like molecules all around it. A molecule at the surface of the liquid experiences greater forces from within the liquid. Thus the molecules at the surface are pulled inward. By contrast, there are **adhesive forces** or the attraction forces between molecules of a solid surface and the molecules of the liquid. The difference in strength between these two forces will determine the behaviour of a liquid and a solid surface.

A **meniscus** is the name for the shape of the surface of a liquid. If you compare a tube of water with a tube of mercury, you will find that the water has a concave or depressed surface, while the mercury has a convex or upward-rising meniscus. This is because the force of adhesion is greater between glass and water than the cohesive force between water molecules, but as you get further from the glass the cohesive forces are greater and they pull the surface down. The situation is reversed with mercury.

Capillary action[13] works to draw water up a tube because the adhesive forces are greater between the tube molecules and the water molecules than the cohesive force between the water molecules. This will continue and the water will rise until the adhesive and cohesive forces are balanced by the weight of the water. The water will rise higher depending on the calibre of the tube. In xylem tubes with small calibre, the water can reach very respectable heights.

The Robotic Pond-Skater Experiment

Here you can demonstrate your inventive or artistic ability to create a robot pond-skater.

REQUIREMENTS

✓ aluminium foil (4 inches x 2 inches)
✓ basin of water or your bath
✓ washing-up liquid

METHOD

Make your robot outline and bend the legs to produce flat shoes. Gently place him on the surface of the water and then drop one drop of washing-up liquid behind him. Watch him skate across the 'pond'.

EXPLANATION

The washing-up liquid breaks the surface tension behind the skater. He is drawn forward because the cohesive forces drag the molecules of water away from the washing-up liquid, and he skates with them.

The robotic skater

The Soap-Powered Boat Experiment

This is very similar and is traditionally done with camphor, but a small piece of your dad's shaving soap will work as well. You can do this in your bath.

REQUIREMENTS

Cut out a boat shape with a hole in the back, into which you put a small pellet of soap. The boat doesn't have to be elaborate, just a triangle if you wish.

METHOD

Settle the boat shape on the water. It will slowly power its way across the bath surface due to the soap-powered motor.

EXPLANATION

The soap breaks the surface tension of the water and works like a little engine to propel the boat across the bath.

The Jet-Boat Experiment

I used to find that the above boat was too slow for my liking, so I used to make this jet-boat.

REQUIREMENTS

- ✓ a metal cigar tube – your uncle may have one (doesn't everyone have an uncle who smokes cigars?)
- ✓ a fizzy tablet – I used to use one that my folks got for headaches, but I mustn't advertise, so any one will probably do. Ask first!

METHOD

Make a hole in the screw-on flat cap. To set it off put the tablet into the cigar tube (you may need to break it up first). Screw the end on then submerge the jet-boat in water. It will soon fizz and jet-propel the boat across the water. Be prepared to rinse the bath out after, since it can leave a crusty foam when the bath is emptied and you will not be popular.

The Floating Needle Experiment

OK, so I said that you can make small metal objects float. You can actually use this as a challenge to your friends. Ask them to make a needle float. They will try and fail miserably, until you show them how!

REQUIREMENTS

- ✓ a sewing needle
- ✓ basin of water
- ✓ small piece of blotting paper

Invite your friends to float the needle. You can even tell them that surface tension will allow it to float, but they will try all sorts of ways to lay it on the water, without success. The problem they will experience is that they will break the surface and it will sink.

Hence the blotting paper! Lay the blotting paper on the surface of the water and then lay the needle of top. Wait a few moments until it soaks with water, then touch it and it will sink, leaving the needle floating – due to surface tension.

The Pepper Challenge

This is another way for you to score over your friends. It's a good one to get them going by offering the challenge, then seeing them fail, before you introduce science to the whole affair.

REQUIREMENTS

✓ small glass or bowl of water
✓ pepper pot

METHOD

Sprinkle pepper over the surface of the water. Challenge your friends to insert their index finger into the bowl or glass, to touch the bottom and

The Pepper trick

then get it out without getting pepper on their finger. Tell them that they are not allowed to put any glove or shield on to their finger.

Having watched them all fail miserably you dip your finger in. Mysteriously the pepper specks will all scatter away from your finger. You take it out – free of pepper – and take a bow.

EXPLANATION

A slight trick. Before you start, rub your finger in your hair. Natural hair oil will cover your finger. Thus, when you put your finger in the water the oil on your finger lowers the surface tension and the water spreads out, taking the pepper with it.

This can be even more effective if you put a drop of washing-up liquid on your finger and dip it in. You might do that after you have explained your trick and the science behind it.

The Magic Circle Experiment

This follows on from the last experiment or challenge. Basically, you have a loop of thread and a bowl of water. You challenge the audience to drop the thread on the water and make a circle of it.

REQUIREMENTS

✓ a thread that you tie into a circle of about two inches diameter
✓ a bowl of water

METHOD

You begin as outlined above. No one will be able to do it. But if you dip your magic finger (already oiled on your hair or with a spot of washing-up liquid) into the middle of the loop and touch the water the thread will immediately form a circle.

EXPLANATION

Again, you lower the surface tension in the middle, so the cohesive forces further out will drag the water molecules in every direction away from your finger. And that will form a magic circle.

The Sands Of Time

This is a magic trick really. You take some sand, drop it into a bowl of water and explain that this is mysterious sand that you collected from the Sahara. It is so old and has not been in touch with water for so long that it never gets wet. Never, ever! And you demonstrate by reaching into the bowl, grabbing a handful and taking it out. You drop it on a plate and your audience can feel it to be … well, as dry as the sands of the desert.

✓ a cupful of sand
✓ a white household candle
✓ an old frying pan that you won't need to use again

Method

Drop the sand into the frying pan and heat it until it is hot enough to scorch a piece of paper that you lay on top of it. Be careful, do not do this unattended and do not allow the paper to ignite. Now add one inch of candle to the sand. Let it melt and then mix it all the way through. Let it cool completely then tap it out on to a covered surface. It will come out as a solid lump, but you can crumble this into a pile of sand. You are ready to begin the above trick, because the sand is coated in wax and is waterproof – thanks to its effect on surface tension.

Chromatography

This is a delightfully colourful thing to do. You can separate food colours or a mix of inks by capillary action.

Requirements
✓ several strips of blotting paper, each about an inch wide
✓ assortment of food colourings or inks
✓ basin of water

Method

Make a spot with several overlapping food colourings or inks about an inch up from one edge of the strip. Place them in the bowl, hanging suspended from a shelf by tape or a frame. You will find that

The sands of time

after ten minutes of so the colours will separate and you will get a sequence of colours spreading up the strips.

EXPLANATION

This is the basis of chromatography, one of the main tools for separating all manner of chemicals in analytical chemistry, biochemical research and forensic science.

NEWTONIAN AND NON-NEWTONIAN FLUIDS

Goodness, there is that name again! As I mentioned in his very own chapter, Sir Isaac Newton seemed to touch so many areas of science and leave his name attached to all sorts of principles, rules and laws.

A **Newtonian fluid** is basically a fluid like water that behaves like a fluid no matter how you agitate or stir it. It will change according to pressure and temperature, but it will flow no matter what forces are directly applied to it. Other fluids behave very differently and under certain conditions will behave quite remarkably. These are called **non-Newtonian fluids**, which thicken or become more viscous when stirred and leave a hole in the middle!

A very simple example of a non-Newtonian fluid is 'gloop', a mixture of cornflour and water. If you mix two cups of cornflour with one of water and mix until it is of the consistency of pancake batter, you will have made

Gloop!

gloop (although you may want to colour it with a drop or two of whatever food colouring you would like to make it).

Now, if you stir this round you will find that it makes a hole. The harder you stir it the harder it is to move, but once you stop it turns very runny again. You can actually scoop it up, squeeze it like dough and it almost turns solid – but only as long as you pressurize or agitate it. As soon as you stop it will turn fluid again and run through your fingers.

This is called **shear-thickening**. This effect can be applied very usefully to fluids used in wheel drive systems. It also accounts for the phenomenon of running on wet sand. If you walk on wet sand it demands a great effort, because you immediately sink in. If you run, it is easier, because the sand will seem thick and solid, from the sudden impact of your running feet.

The opposite of this, called **shear-thinning**, is shown by fluids such as paint, which you want to go smoothly on to a surface and then harden as it is left. Natural examples of this can occur in earthquake zones where solid ground liquefies, or avalanches when ice or snow or even solid ground turns fluid and flows down a mountain.

Then there are other fluids like toothpaste, which has to be squeezed from a tube. As you reach the right **shear pressure** it turns fluid and runs out, only to become partially solid on the brush.

Ketchup is another frustrating example most people will have come across. A bottle will not flow, the ketchup just remains as a semi-solid on the bottom, until you agitate it and then all of a sudden it flows out in a stream to give you far more than you want. This is slightly different from the toothpaste case, since this is an example of **thixotropy**. This is the tendency of certain fluids to become fluid after they have been agitated for a certain time. Curiously, the synovial fluid in human joints behaves like this, as does the fluid inside your muscles. People get stiff joints and don't move about. This makes them stiffer. If they move about the synovial fluid gets looser and the joints become easier to move.

QUICKSAND

You must have seen dozens of films where the hero is stuck in quicksand and the villain laughs as he slowly gets sucked down – until he works out a means of escape. Well, quicksand behaves like a non-Newtonian fluid. It seems semi-solid until it is agitated, then it turns liquid. Further agitation as the hero struggles merely decreases the viscosity.

Although quicksand can be very dangerous, it is not usually as bad as the movie-makers would have you believe. It is rarely more than a few feet deep. True, as a non-Newtonian fluid it will become less viscous as you agitate it, but if you just relax, you will actually float upwards because your body is less dense than the sand. Try to float on your back or get on to your front so that you can lie on the surface, when it will support your weight a lot better. Then very slowly try to monkey crawl or paddle your way out.

So now you know!

The formula for the perfect sandcastle

With all this talk about Newtonian and non-Newtonian fluids, and quicksand, you should have a good idea about the problem of making sandcastles. They are often a question of luck: of being on the right bit of beach at the right time. The sand is either too dry and the castles turn into a pile of sand or too wet and it turns into a sand slurry. But scientists at Bournemouth University have come up with the perfect formula to build the prefect sand castle. It is:

$$0.125 \times S = OW$$

where S is the amount of sand and **OW** is the amount of water.

Actually, that just means eight parts sand to one of water. This will give you a good, sculptable texture of sand for perfect castle-making. But personally, I usually build sand pyramids.

CHAPTER ELEVEN

A LITTLE LIGHT RELIEF

We take light so much for granted these days. At the flick of a switch we light up our homes. Just think of what it would have been like when you did not have that luxury and had to depend on candles. Imagine having to do your homework by candlelight. It is no wonder that people lived their lives 'early to bed and early to rise', to capitalize on the natural light.

A SHORT HISTORY OF CANDLES

We don't know when candles were first invented. The Egyptians were certainly using tallow candles in about 3,000BC and the Romans are said to have been the first to mass produce them with ready-made wicks. Candelabra have been excavated from Pompeii. The Chinese used whale fat candles as long ago as the Qin dynasty, whose first emperor gave his name to China.

In medieval times beeswax was used as a substitute for tallow candles, which burned with a great deal of smoke. The church became a great user of candles and they were adapted to tell the time, as well as to provide illumination.

In England in the eighteenth century candles were taxed and there were two guilds of chandlers, one for tallow candles and one for wax. They were the only people permitted to make candles until 1831. In the 1850s paraffin wax was developed for candle making.

The invention of the light-bulb in

Reading *Frankenstein* is spooky by candlelight

119

1879 by Thomas Edison had a dramatic impact on the candle industry, yet it continues and is likely to always be there, for people simply love candles. Nowadays candles are made from a range of materials, including soy.

CANDLEPOWER

The term candlepower used to be an official measure of the intensity of light. One candlepower was the amount of light emitted by a spermaceti candle (made from a substance obtained from the head of a sperm whale) weighing a sixth of a pound, burning at 120 grains per hour.

In the 1860s Michael Faraday (1791–1867) carried out research into candles and the heat and light that they produced. He analyzed the chemical processes involved, the temperatures obtained and essentially explained the science behind candlepower.

If you look at a candle flame you will see a blue area at the base and a darker cone above the wick, which merges with the intense yellow flame above, which throws out the most light. This intense yellow is surrounded by a slightly paler yellow coat. The temperatures in the various parts of the flame are remarkably high, which is why they are so potentially dangerous and can easily burn you – so always take care with naked flames. Amazingly, the area just above the flame gets up to about 600°C. The temperature rises progressively in the centre of the yellow area to about 1,200°C. The highest temperatures, about 1,400°C, occur at the edge of the yellow.

Candle Experiments
There are some rather nice little impromptu experiments that you can do with candles, so next time you have a candle-lit dinner you can impress the family.

The jumping flame

THE JUMPING FLAME EXPERIMENT

If you gently extinguish a candle flame then hold a lit match or another lit candle above the smoking wick the flame will jump back to re-ignite the extinguished candle.

The wax vapour is full of hydrocarbons, which are flammable. You will ignite a column of wax vapour causing the flame to jump. It is always very impressive.

THE ATTRACTED FLAME EXPERIMENT

If you rub a pencil or a comb on your sleeve and hold it about an inch away from the flame, the flame will be drawn towards the pen or comb, because of static electricity. This causes carbon particles in the flame to be attracted towards the flame.

THE MAGIC BREATH EXPERIMENT

You can follow that little experiment up with this one. You tell the audience that you can blow towards a lit candle and attract its flame towards you. To do this get a playing card or a credit card, hold it about a couple of inches from the flame as if it was a shield. Now blow at the centre of the card and the flame will be drawn towards the card.

This occurs because you are creating a fast stream of air around the sides of the card. This causes reduced pressure on the other side relative to the surroundings, so that the flame is drawn in towards the card and towards you. This is an example of **Bernoulli's Principle**.[14]

Magic breath

THE MAGIC BREATH AND BOTTLE EXPERIMENT

Not content to sit on your laurels, you can then show that you can blow out the candle through a bottle. When people disbelieve you, you take a bottle (or a mug, any round cylinder that would seem to act as a barrier) and hold it between you and the candle flame. Just blow at it and the flame will be extinguished.

This occurs because the bottle provides a streamlined surface, so the air currents from your blow join up, and since the flame is directly in its path, it is extinguished.

THE HEAVY AIR EXPERIMENT

Yet another way to put a candle out. All you need this time is a little carbon dioxide. You can produce some quickly by adding a pinch of sodium bicarbonate to vinegar in a glass. It will fizz, as you know, and produce carbon dioxide. All you have to do is pour some of the gas from the glass (or you can if you want pour the carbon dioxide into another glass so it looks as if you have an empty glass) on to the flame, which will go out.

Carbon dioxide extinguishes the flame (hence its use as in fire extinguishers) and it pours because it is heavier than air.

THE CANDLE SUCKING EXPERIMENT

For this you need a saucer or soup bowl, a small safety candle, a little water and a glass or jar. Light the candle and place it in the centre of the saucer. Now invert the glass or jar and place it over the candle. Quickly pour water outside the glass into the saucer. As the candle burns lower and lower and goes out, the water will be sucked up inside the jar, perhaps even flooding over the candle.

The candle burns the oxygen up and heats the inside of the glass. As the gas and glass rapidly cool, the pressure outside is greater than inside so the outside pressure forces water in, creating the impression that water is being sucked in.

Some Spoon Experiments To Reflect Upon

I can never resist a good trick. Here are some very simple gags and tricks, but they all have serious scientific principles behind them. Firstly, still on the subject of dinner table amusements, you might like to consider a bit of spoon magic.

THE UPSIDE-DOWN YOU

If you look into the concave surface of a spoon you will see yourself – upside down!

You have probably noticed this before, but you may not have noticed all of the things about the upside-down you. They all come about because you are seeing an image from a concave mirror. Firstly, you will see an inverted and back-to-front image of yourself. Secondly, as you come closer to the spoon you will see your image get larger. Thirdly, if you just advance your finger into the concavity you will see that it also gets magnified, but at a certain point the image goes blurred and then it flips over and becomes the right way up.

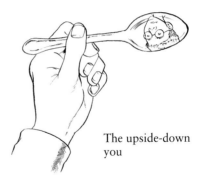

The upside-down you

This is because you have advanced up to the focal point of the mirror. When you are beyond the focal point the image you see is inverted and real; at the focal point it is blurred and no image is seen; closer than the focal point the image is upright, magnified and virtual.

THE SPOON FOCUSING EXPERIMENT

If you put the lights out and shine a torch you will see that it has quite a wide beam. If you shine it at a spoon, the reflected rays will produce a strong narrow beam. This is because the spoon is a concave mirror.

CONCAVE MIRRORS ARE USED ...

- in car headlights, since you want to focus the light
- in shaving mirrors, since if you look close up, within the focal point, you get good magnification
- in reflector telescopes
- in microscopes

THE REDUCED YOU

Now spin the spoon round and look at you in the convex side. You will find a small, distorted you. But the image is always upright. This is a convex mirror.

CONVEX MIRRORS ARE USED ...

- in car mirrors
- in security mirrors in shops
- in wide-angle mirrors at 'blind exits' on roads

THE FORTUNE TELLING SPOON EXPERIMENT

Did you know that you can use the convex surface of a spoon as a divining apparatus, like a crystal ball? You can demonstrate this to folk around the dinner table. You tell them that with the mystic power of the spoon you

The pencil illusion – refraction

can tell where someone you all know is (but who obviously is not at the table with you). Not only that, you can tell what he or she is doing.

No one will believe you, but you can demonstrate. Hold the spoon before you, by the handle so that the convex surface is above your fist. Then advance your other hand with the fingers closed, with the back of your hand pointing towards the ceiling. Touch your third and fourth fingers to the spoon and waggle the first and fifth fingers back and forth, but without straightening them out. A saucy image of your absent friend will appear, as if you have a rear view of them taking a bath!

Refraction Experiments

Refraction is the bending of light when it enters a medium where its speed is different from the medium it entered from. Thus if light enters water from air, it travels slower in water, so the rays will be bent towards the 'normal' of the interface. The normal is perpendicular to the surface. And the reverse situation obviously applies, when light passes from water to air, it will be bent towards the surface. Thus if we place a pencil in water so that it slants, there will be refraction of light as rays come from water to air. The 'apparent' line of sight gives the impression that it is shallower than it is, and the pencil will appear to be bent.

THE APPEARING COIN EXPERIMENT

For this you need an opaque bowl, a copper coin and a jug of water. Place the coin in the bottom of the empty bowl so that you and a spectator can see it. Now ask the spectator to move back so that the coin is hidden by the sides of the bowl. Now you pour water from the jug into the bowl. As the surface of the water becomes visible, so too will the coin. This is due to refraction, as with the pencil.

THE DISAPPEARING COIN EXPERIMENT

This is a good follow-on from the appearing coin, but it is worth preparing it earlier without your spectator being present, so that you can mysteriously make the coin appear.

For this you will need your copper coin, a full glass of water and a saucer. Place the copper coin on the table then place the glass over it, and place the saucer on top of that. You show the spectator the 'empty' glass of water with the saucer on top. Make a few mystic passes, mumble a magic word and remove the saucer to make the coin appear.

Refraction has again made the coin's image appear higher up the glass, but in fact the saucer blocked the image!

THE LIGHT BENDING EXPERIMENT

A very simple way to show how refraction can bend light!

For this you need a shoe box, in which you make a slit through which you can shine a torch, a jar of water and a torch. Position the jar in the box so that when you shine a light through the slit, the beam will strike the jar at an oblique angle. Then turn out the light, switch on the torch and look down into the box. You will see the beam enter the jar and exit it at a different point. You will have bent the light.

As you may remember from the Milky Tyndall Effect Experiment in Chapter Three, water is not a colloid, so you will not be able to see the beam through the jar. If you add a few drops of milk and stir it up, the bent beam should be visible. You can, of course, adjust the position of the jar to alter the difference between entering and exiting beams, or cancel them out so that the beam goes straight through.

NEWTON'S SPECTRUM EXPERIMENT

You can use your shoe box in reverse for this one. Place the torch inside the box and you will produce a slit lamp. Now if you place a prism so that the beam hits one of the angled faces you will see that the emergent light is split into the colours of the rainbow.

This is because refraction through the first surface splits the light into the spectrum, and refraction through the second surface exacerbates the phenomenon to throw out the spectrum. And as you know, you will see the colours in the order red orange, yellow, green, blue, indigo and violet. You can remember it by the mnemonic **R**ichard **O**f **Y**ork **G**ave **B**attle **I**n **V**ain.

TOTAL INTERNAL REFLECTION

This is an unusual but very important phenomenon in optics, for the whole field of fibre optics is based upon it. Total internal reflection occurs when a ray of light strikes a medium surface at an angle larger than a particular critical angle with respect to the normal, or perpendicular to the surface. If the refractive index is lower on the far or potential exiting side of the surface, then no light can pass through and all of the light is reflected. The

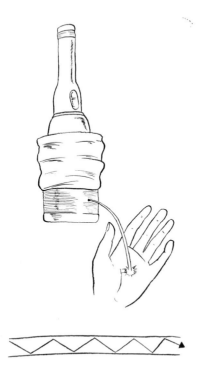

The light fountain

critical angle is the angle above which the total internal reflection occurs.

The Light Fountain Experiment

This is based on a famous experiment first reported in 1842 by the Swiss physicist Daniel Colladon (1802–1893). You literally use water to create a light fountain.

REQUIREMENTS

✓ a torch
✓ an empty tin can
✓ a towel

METHOD

Make a small puncture hole in the side of the can (tap a nail in it) about half an inch from the bottom. Put a piece of tape over the hole, since you want to be able to transport it. Fill the can with water and place it on the edge of the sink, so that when you release the tape the water will spring out sidewards in a thin stream into the sink. This is your fountain. Now switch off the light and aim your torch into the can and put a towel over the top to block any light spilling out. Put your hand under the thin spout of water and you will find that the water fountain has transmitted light into your hand.

EXPLANATION

The light has been totally internally reflected into the jet of water that is spouting out of your fountain.

USES OF FIBRE-OPTICS
• communications
• lighting
• medicine
• archaeology
• rescue work

MAGNIFYING GLASS

The magnifying glass is one of the oldest of all scientific instruments. The ancient Egyptians used crystal chips to magnify objects. The Roman Emperor Nero is said to have had a special ring made with a gemstone lens, which he used when watching actors. Its first use in science was by the friar and philosopher Roger Bacon (c1214–c1294). And of course my old hero, the consulting detective Sherlock Holmes, was never without one when searching for clues that had evaded the eye of mere police inspectors.

Most magnifying glasses have double-convex lenses and are used to magnify objects. This works by placing the lens close to the object under

Sherlock Holmes
always had his
magnifying glass
at the ready

inspection. The light rays are thereby bent toward the centre of the lens. When these bent rays reach the eye they make the object appear much larger than it actually is. If the object is further away, however, the image will flip over so that it is smaller and inverted. The distance at which this flip occurs is twice the focal length (the distance from the optical center of a lens to the point where the light rays converge) of the lens. The magnified image is a virtual image while the smaller, inverted image is a real image.

REAL OR VIRTUAL?

Real Images
- *usually* appear **inverted**
- can be thrown on a screen
- in the case of a mirror, the image lies in front of the reflecting surface
- in the case of a lens, the image lies on the other side of the object

Virtual Images
- *usually* appear **erect**
- cannot be obtained on a screen
- in the case of a mirror, the image lies behind the mirror
- in the case of a lens, the image lies on the same side of the object

The burning glass

At exactly two focal lengths from a piece of paper, the magnifying glass will focus light rays from the sun to produce intense heat, sufficient to ignite the paper. Archimedes is said to have used a burning glass as a weapon in 212BC, when Syracuse was besieged by Marcus Claudius Marcellus, a Roman consul. The Roman fleet was supposedly set on fire.

And of course, the magnifying glass was only the beginning in terms of helping scientists investigate small things. Eventually, this led to the development of the microscope. Which just happens to be the subject of the next chapter.

CHAPTER TWELVE

UNDER THE MICROSCOPE

Sherlock Holmes had been bending for a long time over a low-power microscope. Now he straightened himself up and looked round at me in triumph.

'It is glue, Watson,' said he. 'Unquestionably it is glue. Have a look at these scattered objects in the field!'

I stooped to the eyepiece and focused for my vision.

'Those hairs are threads from a tweed coat. The irregular grey

"It is glue, Watson," said Holmes. "Unquestionably it is glue."

Sherlock Holmes pioneered forensic microscopy!

masses are dust. There are epithelial scales on the left. Those brown blobs in the centre are undoubtedly glue.'

'Well,' said I, laughing, 'I am prepared to take your word for it. Does anything depend upon it?'

'It is a very fine demonstration,' he answered. 'In the St Pancras case you may remember that a cap was found beside the dead policeman. The accused man denies it is his. But he is a picture-frame maker who habitually handles glue.'

'Is it one of your cases?'

'No, my friend, Merivale of the Yard, asked me to look into the case. Since I ran down that coiner by the zinc and copper filings in the seam of his cuff they have begun to realise the importance of the microscope.'

From the opening of 'The Adventure of Shoscombe Old Place'
in *The Case-Book of Sherlock Holmes*
by Sir Arthur Conan Doyle

As I mentioned in the Introduction to this book I was always a fan of the great detective Sherlock Holmes. This scene epitomized the scientific detective to the Victorian and Edwardian reading public. And indeed, the deductive methods of Sherlock Holmes, fictional character though he was, have been used as a blueprint for investigation by several police forces throughout the world. Holmes brought science into his battle against crime.

In 2002 a most unusual ceremony was held outside Baker Street station in London. The Royal Society for Chemistry awarded an 'Extraordinary Honorary Fellowship' to Sherlock Holmes. The conferment of this award was read out to the statue of the great detective that stands, curly pipe in hand, outside the entrance to the station.

Of course, had modern forensic methods been available then, the DNA in the skin epithelial cells that Holmes directed Watson's attention towards would have been matched up with the suspect's own DNA. It is interesting that Sir Alec Jeffries, whose work in the 1980s led to the employment of DNA fingerprinting in criminal investigation, was also honoured by the Royal Society of Chemistry a month previously.

MY OWN MICROSCOPE

I first expressed an ambition to become a doctor when I was six years of age. We had an aged copy of *The Household Doctor* in the family book-case and quite bizarrely I used to spend hours tracing pictures of organs of the body. One evening while I was busily copying a picture of the human skeleton my grandfather asked me if I wanted to be an artist when I grew up, to which I apparently replied, 'No, I can't draw well enough. I think I'll just be a doctor.'

I am not sure if it was quite like that, but my mother always used to embarrass me in front of people with the anecdote. Parents take pleasure in that sort of thing, you know.

Anyway, I digress. The thing is that it was assumed by the family from that moment forward that I would become a doctor. Accordingly, when I passed my O levels and announced that I would be studying Physics, Chemistry and Biology at A level my grandfather duly presented me with a microscope that he had obtained some years before so that I could seriously start studying to become a doctor.

As you may imagine, I felt seriously touched by this, and so I put it to good use. Although I ended up using a multiplicity of microscopes in various laboratories at medical school, I only ever considered them as

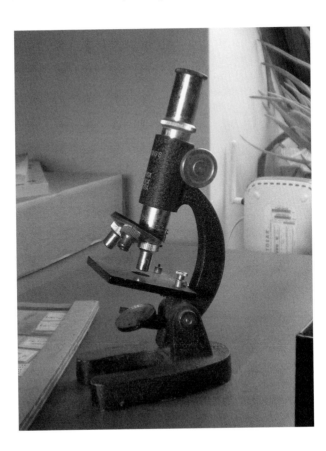

My friend, my microscope

tools. My own microscope became a great friend and with it I looked at all sorts of stuff from stagnant ponds to scales from the wings of moths. I cannot claim to have made any startling discovery with it, but I have learned much from the world that it opens up.

And if you obtain a good microscope I am sure that you will see how much fun science can be.

THE HISTORY OF THE MICROSCOPE

Several early simple instruments were designed in the Netherlands in the late sixteenth century, but it was not until Galileo Galilei invented a compound microscope with a convex and a concave lens in 1609 that it became of any real value. Galileo called his instrument the *occhiolino*, or the 'little eye'. In 1624 he presented his occhiolino to Prince Federico Cesi, president of the Lincean Academy, the first scientific academy in Italy. Since the academy had already received a telescope from Galileo (and had given it the name 'telescope') Giovanni Faber, a botanist and fellow member of the academy, coined the term microscope for it, from the Greek words *micron*, meaning 'small', and *skopein*, meaning 'to look at'.

Marcelo Malpighi (1628–1694) was an Italian doctor who saw the potential of the microscope and began to study the skin, blood vessels and sections of organs such as the liver. His studies of the lungs of the frog were to prove of immense importance, as we shall see in the chapter on Your Amazing Body.

Antonie van Leeuwenhoek (1632–1723) was a Dutch draper and amateur scientist who has a good claim to be the 'father of microbiology'. This quite remarkable man made over 400 microscopes of varying complexity in his life, of which only about 9 have survived. He subjected everything that he could think of (including his own bodily fluids and scrapings from his teeth) to microscopic examinations and submitted his findings to the Royal Society in London. He was the first person to discover microbial organisms, which he called 'animalcules'. He described protozoa (unicellular animals), bacteria, yeast cells, red blood cells and spermatozoa.

A contemporary of his, Robert Hooke (1635–1703), an English architect, physicist and curator of experiments at the Royal Society, also did pioneering work with the microscope. In his book entitled *Micrographia*, published in 1665, he included a series of beautifully illustrated pictures of the miniature world that he saw through his microscope. Among these were pictures of the compound eye of a fly and the first depiction of a plant cell. Indeed, he was the first person to use the word 'cell' in a biological sense, since he likened its appearance to that of a monk's cell, from the Latin *cella*, meaning 'small room'.

The compound microscope was invented by Joseph Jackson Lister in 1830. Effectively, by using several weak lenses at certain distances, the problem of chromatic aberration (which was also a problem in early tele-scopes) could be overcome.

In 1931 Max Knoll and Ernst Ruska invented the electron microscope. As the name implies it uses electrons to produce an image rather than light. This works by speeding up electrons in a vacuum until their wavelength is incredibly small. A stream of them is then fired at the object under study. If this is a cell, then they are absorbed or scattered by the cell's structures to produce an image on an electron-sensitive photographic plate.

In 1932 Frits Zernike invented the phase-contrast microscope, which allowed for the examination of transparent biological materials. No staining was necessary to do this, so living tissue or cells could be studied. Two decades later he was awarded the Nobel Prize in Physics for this invention.

STARTING OFF

There are many excellent beginners' microscopes available. You don't need to spend a lot of money, but do get a kit that includes slides, cover slips, fixatives and the microscope itself. Then the world is literally your oyster. You can start examining it at the microscopic level.

Follow in Hook's footsteps

This is not a bad place to start. All you need to do is cut as fine a slice of cork as you can. Put it in a wet mount, which means place a drop of water on your slide, then with forceps lay the slice of cork on top of the water. Angle a cover slip so that the edge touches the water, then lower the slip on to the slide. Try not to catch any air bubbles. The water should form a seal and then you just get a piece of tissue paper or kitchen paper and touch the edge of the cover slip, which will mop up any excess. Now, have a look at Hook's 'cells'.

Brownian motion

Robert Brown (1773–1858) described what seemed to be spontaneous erratic movement of pollen grains and moss spores when he was studying them under a microscope. In actual fact you can see this phenomenon with all sorts of particles when they are suspended in liquid or gas.

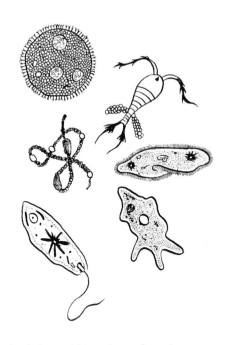

A whole world in a drop of pond water

Try looking at the fat globules in milk. Look at them with 10x objective and work upwards, with whatever magnification you have. It is fascinating.

Pond water

This truly opens up a whole new world. You will probably see single-celled protozoans, like amoeba, slipper-shaped paramecium and flagellated euglena. The latter, incidentally, has both animal and plant features: it can move by a whip-like flagellum, absorb food particles like an animal, yet has choloroplasts with which it can photosynthesize.

You will also see algae and Volvox colonies, and creatures like the multi-cellular Rotifera, which are higher up the evolutionary ladder. They are wheel-like, have tiny hairs and are fascinating to watch. And, much bigger, you may see Cyclops, the water fleas, which dash around eating algae. And there is much more to see.

Feathers, moss, ferns and leaves

These are all worth subjecting to microscopical scrutiny. Indeed, the more you look at, the more you will understand the Eureka moments that people like Antonie van Leeuwenhoek, Robert Hooke and Robert Brown must have experienced when they saw the microscopic world for the first time.

Human cells

You cannot call yourself a microscopist worth your salt until you have looked at some of your own cells under the microscope. The simplest ones are readily available from the inside of your cheek.

These cells are called **squamous epithelial cells**. To collect them just get a lolly stick and gently scrape the inside of your cheek. The cells come away very easily and you don't have to exert any real pressure. Then smear this on a slide and with a cover slip drag an edge over the smear. This will make it very thin. Then let it dry for a few minutes. You will probably have some methylene blue in your microscope kit, so just add a drop to the smear, which will make the cells stand out. Drop the cover slip on top and give yourself a microscopic inspection – figuratively speaking.

CHAPTER THIRTEEN

THROUGH THE TELESCOPE

I have always been a dabbler in astronomy. My interest was kindled by watching *The Sky at Night*, an amazing television programme that started in 1957, and which has been almost continuously presented by Sir Patrick Moore. He is in my mind a national treasure and the greatest popularizer of science that Britain has ever had. He certainly sparked my enthusiasm

Sir Patrick Moore

for science, and I am quite sure stimulated many thousands of people to take up a scientific or related career.

A SHORT HISTORY OF ASTRONOMY

At one time people believed in a flat earth. This view gradually changed and it was realized that the earth was a sphere. Yet it was thought that it occupied a central position in the universe, with the sun, the moon and the stars circling it, all attached to the dome of the heavens. This geocentric (earth at the centre) model was put forward by Ptolemy of Alexandria (AD90–168) in a book he wrote called *Almagest*, or *The Great Treatise*. It would remain the dominant model of the universe for centuries. A significant part of this theory, of course, was the observation that there were 'five wanderers', or five objects that moved markedly across the sky, unlike the relatively stationary stars. These were the planets, which were named after the gods: Mercury, Venus, Mars, Jupiter and Saturn.

Nicolaus Copernicus (1473–1543), a priest, physician, mathematician and astronomer, postulated that this was not the case. In a book entitled *De revolutionibus orbium coelestium* (*On the Revolutions of the Celestial Spheres*), published shortly before his death, he gave a detailed mathematical analysis, which proposed that the earth actually revolved around the sun rather than the other way round. In other words, he suggested a heliocentric system.

Tycho Brahe (1546–1601) is one of the most colourful characters in the history of science. He was a Danish nobleman who lost part of his nose in a duel when he was a student. Because of this, he studied medicine and alchemy, which enabled him to construct a false nose of silver and gold, which he held in place with a special paste or glue. In 1572 he observed what seemed to be a new star in the constellation Cassiopeia. He observed this and wrote a small book entitled *De Nova Stella*, thereby giving us the word 'nova' for a new star. This discovery was the start of a lifelong observation of the heavens. Assisted by Jepp, his court jester (whom he thought to have the gift of second sight, and who sat by his feet during meals), he produced a set of data that was to prove crucial to further development.

Yet although Tycho Brahe was intrigued by Copernicus's heliocentric system he did not believe it himself. Instead he proposed a compromise that allowed for some of his observations. This was a geo-heliocentric system, in which he suggested that the sun and the moon orbited the earth, but the other planets orbited the sun.

Johannes Kepler (1571–1630) was a German mathematician and astronomer. For a while he worked with Tycho Brahe as an assistant, until political and religious difficulties forced him to leave. He fundamentally disagreed with Brahe's geo-heliocentric model, believing instead that the heliocentric system had to be the correct one. Indeed, having had access to Brahe's data, he was able to make a significant contribution to the field of astronomy – Kepler's three laws of planetary motion. These state that:

1 The orbit of every planet is an ellipse with the sun at a focus
2 A line joining a planet and the sun sweeps out equal areas during equal intervals of time
3 The square of the orbital period of a planet is directly proportional to the cube of the semi-major axis of its orbit

Galileo Galilei (1564–1642) was an Italian astronomer, philosopher, mathematician and physicist, one of the key figures in the scientific revolution. Indeed, it has been said that he almost single-handedly brought about a revolution in scientific thinking. Galileo originally planned to become a priest, but instead began training in medicine at the University of Pisa. While there he changed his mind again and began to study mathematics and philosophy. How fortunate the world was that he made that decision, for it equipped him to begin to unravel many of the mysteries of the universe.

His many discoveries were remarkable. He developed the compass, advanced many of the theories of physics and raised observational astronomy to a new level. He was one of the first astronomers to use a telescope,[15] a relatively simple 20x refractor, which was sophisticated enough for him to observe and describe the phases of Venus, map the moon and coin the term 'crater'. In addition, he described sunspot activity in the sun and discovered the four largest moons of Jupiter.

His work effectively confirmed the theory of Copernicus that the sun was at the centre of the solar system, rather than the earth. He published his findings in 1610, but immediately drew the wrath of the Roman Inquisition. In 1632 he was forced by the Inquisition to recant and was then kept under house arrest until his death in 1642.

Sir Isaac Newton (1643–1727), the great omni-scientist, was interested in optics, astronomy, mathematics and many other areas of science. In his theory of universal gravitation he showed mathematically that the motions of objects on the earth were behaving under the influence of a force, just as were the planets. Effectively, he proved that Kepler's laws were correct.

Newton also solved one of the problems of refractor telescopes. This was a phenomenon known as chromatic aberration. By building a reflecting telescope, using mirrors rather than lenses, he removed the problem and began the technology that would allow astronomers to see further into deep space.

Sir William Herschel (1738–1822) was an astronomer, telescope maker and composer. He discovered the planet Uranus, several of its moons and the existence of infra-red radiation. During his life he constructed over 400 telescopes, including a 40-foot giant. A complete genius, he also composed 24 symphonies.

The twentieth and twenty-first centuries of course have seen huge advances in astronomy. In 1957 the Lovell Telescope, a radio-telescope, was constructed at Jodrell Bank observatory in Cheshire. It was the largest dish telescope in the world at the time, and is currently the third largest, after the Green Bank radio-telescope in West Virginia, USA and the Effelsberg radio-telescope in Bonn in Germany.

The Hubble Space Telescope was carried into space by a space shuttle in 1990. It is serviced from time to time by teams of astronauts. It is supplying scientists with data that is constantly pushing back the frontiers of knowledge. It will soon be replaced by an even more sophisticated space telescope.

SO, WHERE ARE WE IN THE SCHEME OF THINGS?

The heavens are vast! The distance between stars is far too great to consider measuring in miles or kilometres. The light-year is the measure of distance used. This is the distance that light travels in one year. And if you consider that light travels at the speed of 186,000 miles per second, you can get some idea of the distance involved. Our very nearest star (apart from the sun) is Centauri C or Proxima Centauri, which is 4.3 light years away.

Astronomers also use a measure called a parsec, but that is really getting more technical that we need here.

The earth is one planet of the nine in the solar system. This in turn is a dot on the edge of the Milky Way, a medium-sized saucer-like galaxy, which contains something like two to four hundred billion stars. In its turn, the Milky Way is only one of the billions of galaxies that make up the universe. Space goes on an awfully long way.

MAPPING THE SKY

Although we live in a heliocentric system, in order to make any sense of the sky we have to use a geocentric model. This means that you have to place the earth at the centre and look at everything else in the sky as if they are moving relative to us. Thus, the sun is seen to have an orbit round the earth. And it takes a year to complete one orbit.

The celestial sphere is imagined as a huge sphere concentric with the

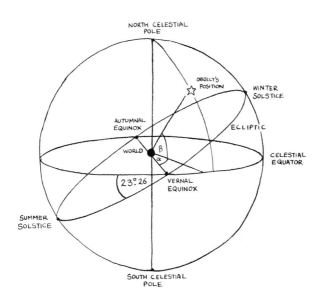

The celestial sphere

earth and rotating on the same axis. Its equator is the same as the earth's equator, so that it is divided into a northern and a southern hemisphere.

The ecliptic is the name given to the apparent path of the sun on this celestial sphere. It makes an angle of 23° 26'. Thus, the intersection of these two great circles, the celestial equator and the ecliptic, is marked by two diametrically opposite points – the **equinoxes**. These are observed twice a year – the vernal (spring) equinox and the autumn equinox – when the night and the day are the same length.

And note that there are two points when they are maximally apart. These represent the solstices. In the northern hemisphere the winter solstice marks the shortest day, when the sun is at its highest point on the ecliptic, and the summer solstice marks the longest day, when it is at its lowest point. The two are reversed for an observer in the southern hemisphere, of course.

STONEHENGE – AN ANCIENT OBSERVATORY?

Every year people flock to Stonehenge and other megalithic sites at the solstices and equinoxes to try to capture the magic of the place. Since the 1970s an archaeo-astronomical theory has arisen which suggests that these sites were actually Stone Age observatories designed to pin-point the solstices and equinoxes, for they would have had significance for agriculture. And of course, since the heavenly bodies would have been considered deities, there is no reason to think that they were not also places of worship.

With the naked eye on a clear night you can see about 2,000 stars. There are about 30 especially bright stars that are worth looking out for. These include Sirius, Vega and Polaris, the Pole Star.

To make sense out of the sky we look out for known collections, the **constellations**. From earth there are 88 constellations, about 60 of which can be seen from northern latitudes.

Now at this point it is worth being aware that what we tend to think of as constellations are not strictly speaking the same thing that a serious astronomer would mean. Correctly speaking, a constellation is an area of the sky containing the stars and all of the objects in that area of space. What most people talk about are really just groups of stars that have a recognizable pattern, such as the Plough. Astronomers call these patterns **asterisms**. For our purposes I will stick with the asterisms, for those are the ones that you will recognize most easily. When you have seen those and can recognize them, then you will be able to work your way around the sky. It will be the framework on which you can build.

So, it is worth getting a simple star atlas and familiarizing yourself with half a dozen or so of these to begin with. I would suggest looking out for: Plough, Little Plough (also called Little Bear), Dragon (also called Draco), Cassiopeia, Great Bear (Ursa Major), Orion.

You will have heard of the signs of the Zodiac. This is more to do with astrology than astronomy, but remember that up until the Renaissance the two were virtually considered the same subject. Suffice it to say that the Zodiac belt is the name given to the constellations that follow the path of the ecliptic. These are worth checking out on a star atlas, especially when you come to observing meteorite showers, which we will come to shortly.

Start with Polaris

To get your bearings you need to find the Pole Star. This is the North Star and it has a fixed position in the sky. To find it seek out the Plough and follow an imaginary line from the two stars at the end farthest from the handle. These are the pointer stars, and about five times the distance between the two pointers, you will find a bright star. This is Polaris, the Pole Star. You are now looking due north. Looking up at the sky from England you would expect to see it about half-way up the sky. If you measured the angle between, it would give you your latitude. But for that you would need an astrolabe.

Sounds like time for a practical experiment.

Make Your Own Astrolabe

An astrolabe is an instrument of considerable history. The name comes from the Greek *astrolabon*, meaning 'star-taker'. It was used by astronomers, astrologers and navigators. It had many uses including locating and predicting the positions of the sun, moon, the planets and stars. It was also used for surveying and telling the time.

Traditional astrolabes were quite complex devices that were best used on *terra firma*, or dry land. They were not suited to the rolling and heaving of a ship, so the mariner's astrolabe was devised to measure latitude. And you can make a simple one right now to test out on the next clear night.

REQUIREMENTS

✓ a protractor
✓ a drinking straw
✓ Sellotape
✓ string
✓ a nut or bolt

METHOD

Invert the protractor and tie the string to the flat part so that it hangs down immediately below the 90°. You may need to make a hole in your protractor. Tie the nut or bolt to the other end so that it will act as a plumb bob. Attach the straw to the base of the protractor, just above the point where the string hangs. You are ready.

Just a straw, a
protractor and a
plumb bob

Go outside and locate the Pole Star, then view it through the drinking straw. The line of the string will give you the angle it makes with the 90° line. This angle gives you the angle of the Pole Star above the horizon at the point you are observing from. This is the latitude of the point.

Make An Umbrella Planetarium

This really is a worthwhile exercise if you want to understand the night sky. As you know, the Pole Star is a fixed star. All of the other stars wander round this pole of the celestial sphere in an anti-clockwise direction once every 24 hours (actually every 23 hours and 56 minutes).

REQUIREMENTS

✓ an umbrella (and permission to use it)
✓ a pack of star stickers (if you can, get glow-in-the-dark ones)

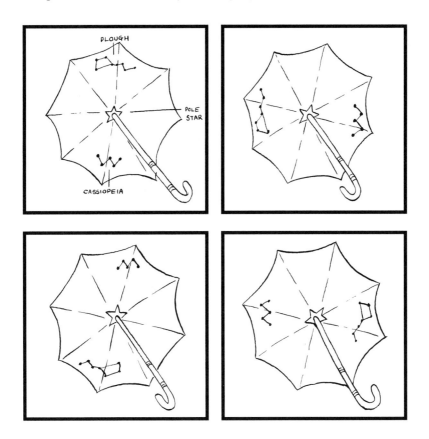

An umbrella makes a fine planetarium

METHOD

Go out on a clear night and, with the umbrella up, point the end at the Pole Star, so that the handle is pointing directly at you. So, the apex of the umbrella represents the Pole Star. Look through the umbrella and you may be able to see some of the bright stars through the material. Put stickers over them, so that you can then 'see' the constellations (or asterisms). Put as many as you can recognize. Make sure that you put the Plough and Cassiopeia to begin with. They are good landmarks.

Most umbrellas have eight sections. In 24 hours the stars will sweep anti-clockwise round the Pole Star, so each section represents three hours, and each quarter represents six hours. By rotating through each quarter turn, you can see which constellations are where, even if you can't see them, but you will be able to predict where they are on subsequent nights.

So there you are. You have a means of mapping the sky and understanding what is happening up there.

(Of course, if there is an old umbrella heading for the dustbin, then you could make holes instead of using stickers. When you go inside and switch on the lights, then you will have your own lit-up planetarium to view. This is not recommended if the umbrella is going to be used as protection against the rain.)

GETTING STARTED

OK, now you have an idea about the sky, so it is time to start looking. The first thing is to consider what you use. The impulse may be to go out and buy the biggest, most expensive telescope that you can. My advice is not to. You have to consider your needs, your means and what exactly you are going to start observing. It is very much a case of using the right instrument for the type of observations you plan to make.

Naked-eye observing

That's right: just using your unaided eyes. If you have read through the chapter you will already realize that the early astronomers used no aids yet made sufficiently accurate observations to be able to make predictions. Just consider the megalithic monument makers, for instance.

There are three types of body that you can begin observing with your naked eye – the moon, comets and meteorite showers. I will leave the moon for now, since you will gain a lot more by looking at it through binoculars or a telescope, yet once you have read the rudiments that I will give you, you can see what you can glean with the naked eye.

Comets are huge chunks of water, ice, rock and space debris. As they approach the sun they vaporize, leaving those characteristic tails. They vary in size from a few hundred metres across to several kilometres. I have said that you might see them with the naked eye, but I warn you, you either need a lot of luck or you need to know when to look out for them. On average you can see a comet with the naked eye every five years or so! You really need to check up when they are about to appear and then make sure you are looking at the right part of the sky. But you never know, you might see one, and get to have a comet named after yourself.

Comets come from two areas, called the **Kuiper Belt** and the **Oort Cloud**. The Kuiper Belt is a vast icy area that stretches from Neptune out and beyond Pluto.[16] Comets from this area are considered to be 'short-period' comets, since they orbit the sun in a relatively short (in astronomical terms) time. Halley's Comet[17] is the most famous of the short-period comets (classified as any comet with an orbit of less than 200 years). It has an orbit of about 75 years.

The Oort Belt is more of a spherical cloud that actually surrounds the solar system. It produces about 10 trillion comets! They are called 'long-period' comets, since they take a long time to orbit the sun. The Hale-Bopp comet is such a comet, with an orbit of over 2,500 years. It was independently discovered in 1995 by two observers, Alan Hale, an experienced observer of some 200-odd comets, using his telescope from his drive, and Thomas Bopp, seeing his first comet.

Meteorites are relatively small chunks of rock, metal or other debris that result from the debris from comets' tails burning up in the atmosphere. Effectively, it is because the earth moves through the trail of tail debris that this happens. From the earth you will see them as bright flashes or 'shooting stars' in the sky.

Meteorite showers can be spotted at several times of the year and are the best things to see with the naked eye. It is because the earth regularly crosses these trails that you will see them at predictable times. During some of these showers you may see a hundred or so per hour.

The fascinating thing about these showers is that the meteors all seem to erupt from the same point in the

Look for the radiant of the meteor shower

sky. This is called the **radiant**. Spotting this may just be the thing that hooks you on astronomy for life.

Each of the meteorite showers is named after the constellation that they appear from. The following are just a few of the showers that you may like to 'keep an eye out' for!

SHOWER	DATES	
Quadrantids	28 December – 3 January	Named after extinct constellation Quadrans muralis
Perseids	23 July – 29 August	Named after the constellation Perseus
Orionids	15–29 October	Named after the constellation Orion
Leonids	13–20 November	Named after constellation Leo
Geminids	6–19 December	Named after constellation Gemini

Binoculars or telescope?

This is not an 'either or' sort of question. Both have their pros and cons. If you have not previously used an instrument to observe the skies then binoculars are a good start. They have so many uses and if you find that you want to go further, I would suggest that you then consider a small telescope.

A consideration of the optics involved can be quiet technical, so I am keeping this as simple as possible.

Binoculars   These essentially consist of a pair of mirror-symmetrical telescopes aligned together to give the viewer binocular vision. Very early binoculars (and many cheap varieties, including opera glasses) were based on Galilean optics. This used a convex objective lens and a concave eyepiece lens. This has the advantage of giving the viewer an upright image. It has the disadvantage of having a very narrow field of view and not very much magnification.

More sophisticated binoculars will give a wider field and greater magnification with correction of the image, so that you see the object as it looks with the naked eye, only much clearer and bigger. Generally they will be labelled 8 x 40, 7 x 50 or 10 x 50. The first number is the magnification and the second is the aperture of the front lenses. The latter two will be quite adequate for most sky-watching.

The beauty of the binoculars is that you can sweep the sky with a wide angle and quickly focus in on things. They are very transportable, of course, and easier to whip out than a telescope.

But hand tremor is a problem with them. No matter how steady you think you are, when you are looking at distant objects in space you may find this is another matter. A tripod may be worth obtaining so that you can fix and steady.

Telescopes   There are basically two types, the refractor and the reflector. The refractor uses lenses to collect and refract or bend the light to a focus. The reflector uses a curved mirror to reflect light to the viewer.

The refractors came first and are still incredibly useful. Galileo used a 20x refractor and opened up the mysteries of the sky, so you can see how effective they can be. But they have a disadvantage in that they can produce the phenomenon of chromatic aberration. That means that you can see coloured rings about objects and obscure their view. Very simply, this is because the lenses refract the different wavelengths of light by differing amounts to split the light into a rainbow effect. Newton studied this, of course, and invented the reflector telescope to get round the problem.

The reflector as designed by Newton had the eyepiece on top of the telescope.

Galileo's telescope in the Institute and Museum of the History of Science in Florence

Sir Patrick Moore's 15-inch reflector telescope

Essentially, a reflector telescope has a concave mirror at one end. This mirror collects light from the astronomical bodies and shines it on to a flat mirror. This reflects the light up through the lenses of the eyepiece, so that a view of stars is seen that cannot be seen with the naked eye.

Sir Patrick Moore's 5-inch refractor telescope

My trusty
telescope

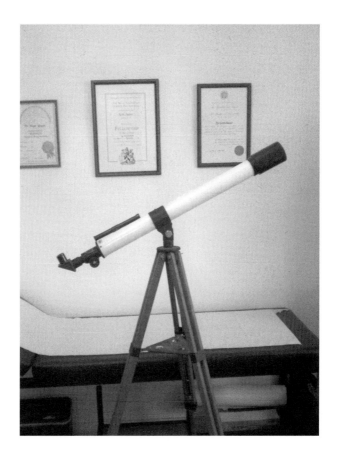

But there are now other ways of dealing with this nuisance and it is worth seeking advice before shelling out a great deal of money on an expensive telescope.

Generally, telescopes with a small aperture (75 millimetres or less) will probably be refractors.

Do note, however, that telescopes will reverse your image and so you have to get used to this. It is a different view from that with the binoculars. But on the other hand, you will be able to see deeper into space.

Moon watching

This is great fun. Every child knows about 'the man in the moon', and will have been amazed at the face that can be seen. Yet once you train a set of binoculars or a telescope on the moon you will rekindle that sense of awe.

Again, I must emphasize that binoculars will give you a straightforward view, whereas the telescope may confuse you at first with its reversed image. The other thing that may confuse you when you look at a moon map is that east and west will generally relate to the directions as if you were standing on the moon itself, for they are its east and west, not those of the earth.

The moon orbits the earth every 27.3 days. It is in synchronous motion, meaning that it effectively only has one face turned to the earth at any time. As a result, there was endless speculation and not a few science fiction tales over the years about what was on the 'dark side of the moon'. In fact, it was photographed by the Soviet probe Luna 3 in 1959.

Let us consider the main features that you can see on the moon. Once again, you will see that it was Galileo Galilei who led the way, for on 30 November 1609 he trained his telescope on the moon. To his surprise, he found that the moon was not a smooth sphere, but had both mountains and cup-like depressions that he called 'craters', from the Latin for cup.

Bear that in mind when you start your own moon watching.

Craters   The moon is pock-marked by the impact craters of asteroids, comets and meteorites. About half a million of these craters are one kilometre or more in diameter, and there is a multiplicity of much smaller ones. Indeed, moon rocks retrieved by the Apollo Project have shown tiny craters upon them.

Over the years they have been named. You can get large lunar maps with them all listed, but as a taster look at this simple drawing, which shows the positions of some of the main craters. On your first observations of a full moon you may get a buzz when you look at Ptolemaeus, Plato, Copernicus, Tycho Brahe and Kepler. They are all names that you will recognize from reading this book.

Terrae and Montes   The lighter areas on the moon are the highlands, called the terrae, which include the montes, or the mountains of the moon. Some of the mountain ranges border on some of the larger impact craters. Indeed, it is thought that they may actually represent the walls of some ancient craters. This is quite different from the mountains of the earth, which were formed by tectonic activity.

Look for the lunar Alps nearby the Plato crater.

Mares   These are very apparent from earth with the naked eye. You will see them as darker, seemingly featureless areas. Ancient astronomers thought these were seas, and they were named accordingly. Look on my map then have a go yourself at seeing the following seas, starting in the west: Ocean of Storms (*Oceanus Procellarum*), Sea of Rains (*Mare Imbrium*), Sea of Serenity (*Mare Serenitatis*), Sea of Crises (*Mare Crisium*), Sea of Tranquility (*Mare Tranquillitatis*) and Sea of Fecundity (*Mare Fecunditatis*).

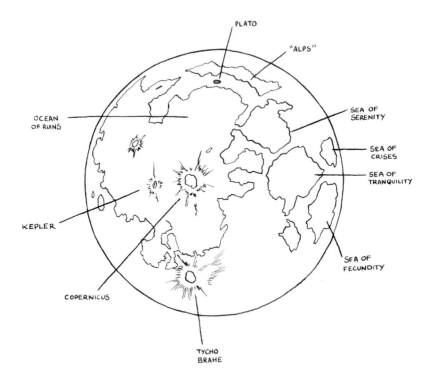

A rough map of the moon

It was at a point on the south west of the Sea of Tranquility on 20 July 1969 that the first manned landing on the moon was made. The Apollo 11 mission commanded by Neil Armstrong made history when the lunar module Eagle touched down, carrying Armstrong and 'Buzz' Aldrin. The point they landed at was called Tranquility Base. Neil Armstrong was the first man to walk on the moon and 'Buzz' Aldrin was the second. The third member of the mission, Michael Collins, remained in orbit around the moon while his companions carried out their famous investigations. I vividly recall watching those historic moments on TV.

Three small craters to the north of the base have been named Aldrin, Collins and Armstrong after the astronauts.

Curiously the 'darker side' of the moon has no mares at all.

Phases of the moon, the orbit and the lunar month

The phases of the moon are interesting. They are caused by the changing illumination from the sun as the moon orbits the earth. The orbit around the earth, from start position to finish position, takes 27.3 days. A point of confusion, however, is the lunar month, which takes 29.5 days. This is because a lunar month is the time taken to reach the same phase. Since the earth is orbiting the sun, the moon will travel more than 360° to reach the same phase.

Each of the 12 full moons traditionally has a name, depending on what time of the year they appear. For example, a January full moon is called an 'Old Moon', a May full moon is a 'Planting Moon', a September full Moon is a 'Harvest Moon'.

A blue moon is used to describe the occasion when you have two full moons in a month. The term was first used by an astronomer in 1946, although the phenomenon of an extra full moon has been known about for millennia. The Greek astronomer Meton of Athens described this extra full moon in about 2,500BC. He noticed that in a nineteen-year period there would be seven more full moons than calendar months. Thus, there are seven extra full moons in the so-called Metonic cycle of nineteen years, meaning that you can expect a blue moon at some stage about every two and a half years.

The moon has been observed to be blue at various times in the past, and sometimes even green. This will only happen when there is a great deal of atmospheric pollution, such as after a cataclysmic volcanic eruption. Back in 1883 when the volcano on the Indonesian island of Krakatoa erupted with devastating effect – the so-called 'bang that was heard around the world' – the moon did appear green for a short period and then blue for two years.

The reason is similar to the little milk experiment that I described in Chapter Three. Particles of about one micron were spewed into the atmosphere from the volcano. This size is just right to scatter red wavelengths of light, but allow the rest to pass through. Thus moonlight, or the reflected light from the sun off the moon, was affected to make it look blue. Interestingly, it is recorded that the sun at times looked lavender colour after the Krakatoa eruption.

In areas subject to other sudden atmospheric pollution, such as occurs when there are forest fires, the moon can appear pink or even red. This is because the particles in the atmosphere are considerably smaller than one micron, so red light waves are not scattered, but blue ones are.

Planet watching

Of the planets in the solar system, five can be seen from the earth with the naked eye or with binoculars or telescope. These are Mercury, Venus, Mars, Jupiter and Saturn.

Mercury is the hardest of all to see, being so close to the sun. Three times a year it can be seen for a few weeks in the twilight hours, and three more times a year in the early morning light.

Venus is the brightest of the objects in the sky, which is helpful. Look to see this planet close above the western horizon after sunset. It is misnamed the 'evening star'. Or you can see it above the eastern horizon in the morning as the equally misnamed 'morning star'.

You will have heard about planets going retrograde. Effectively, at times they seem to slow down in their orbit and then go backwards for a while before going back into regular orbit. This was noticed by the ancients and was a real puzzle for them. It only became clear when Copernicus came up with his explanation about a heliocentric system. Mercury is the planet

that exhibits retrograde motion most often. And of course, the planets do not go backwards, it is all to do with the shape of their orbits, the speed that they are going relative to the earth.

Jupiter is the next brightest and it can be high or low at any time of the night, always around the ecliptic. Look due south in the early evening to spot it. It sets earlier and earlier each night until January when it may be hard to spot at twilight. With your telescope you may just be able to see some of its moons.

Mars varies in brightness depending on where it is in its orbit. Look for its red colour, for it is the 'red planet'. You may have heard of the 'canals of Mars'. These were linear tracks visible to Victorian astronomers and were thought to be waterways or routes built by Martians. This idea was first put forward after the famous Italian astronomer Giovanni Schiaparelli in 1877 called them '*canali*', meaning channels. He was misinterpreted and hence the idea that Mars was an inhabited planet grasped the public imagination. It was finally discredited in 1965 when NASA's Mariner 4 failed to demonstrate any evidence of life, and beamed home pictures of a barren landscape pocked with impact craters.

Saturn is also possible to see in the night, and its rings will make you wonder! But it isn't always around at convenient times. It will appear faintly yellowish.

And that is it.

Happy observing!

CHAPTER FOURTEEN

MAGNETISM AND ELECTRICITY

The ancients were aware that a lodestone, a naturally occurring piece of the mineral magnetite, could attract pieces of iron. Not only that, but if it was suspended by a thread it would mysteriously point to the north. Understandably, this was of incredible benefit as a means of navigation. The word 'lodestone' comes from the Middle English meaning 'leading stone'. It is thought that the word magnet comes from the fact that lodestones were mined in Magnesia in Greece.

The ancient Greeks made rudimentary investigations into magnetism, as did the ancient Chinese, yet no major work was done on it until the end

My lodestone

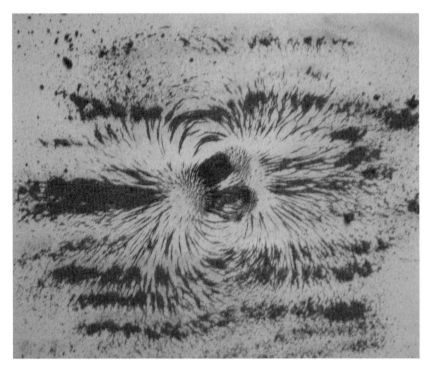

You can show a magnetic field with iron filings

of the sixteenth century, when Queen Elizabeth I's personal physician Dr William Gilbert (1544–1603) carried out research over eighteen years. His reason for doing so was because it had been thought for centuries that magnets had healing powers. He completely disproved all this and began a systematic investigation of their properties.

In 1600 he published his findings in a book entitled *De Magnete, Magneticisque Corporibus, et de Magno Magnete Tellure* (*On the Magnet and Magnetic Bodies, and on the Great Magnet the Earth*). This is widely regarded as the first truly scientific book to be printed in England. It is usually just referred to as *De Magnete*.

Gilbert was an ingenious experimenter. He believed that the earth was in fact a giant magnet, and so he created a small sphere of lodestone, which he called a *terrella*. Knowing that a magnetized needle acted as a compass, always pointing north, he found that if one was held near his *terrella* it would deviate and point to a 'pole' of the *terrella*. He was able to come to several conclusions, which really formed the basis of the main facts that we know about magnets.

MAGNET FACTS

- the earth behaves like a giant magnet
- a magnet has two poles, a north and a south
- if suspended, the north pole of a magnet will point to the north pole of the earth, and the south pole of the magnet will point to the south pole of the earth
- like poles repel one another, while opposites attract
- potentially magnetic substances, such as iron nails or steel needles, can be magnetized or turned into a magnet when a magnet is rubbed on them
- a magnet is surrounded by a magnetic field
- if a bar magnet is cut in half it will form two separate magnets with their own poles

STATIC ELECTRICITY

The ancient Greeks had also been aware of the curious phenomenon of static electricity. Thales of Miletus (c625–c545BC), a mathematician and philosopher, discovered that if amber was rubbed with fur it would attract light objects, like straw or feathers. He assumed that it was another example of magnetism.

Dr William Gilbert was very interested in this phenomenon when he came to study magnetism and wrote about it in his book. He concluded that it was a different effect entirely. Since the Greek word for amber was '*electron*' he called this effect '*electricus*', from which the word 'electricity' was derived.

What actually happens is that a build-up of electrical charge, either positive (+) or negative (-), occurs on the surface of objects. This will stay there until they are either earthed, or they are discharged. Effectively, the surface atoms on the surface of the object either have too few electrons and have a positive (+) charge, or too many and have a negative (-) charge.

If two similarly charged objects are brought close they will repel each other. Opposites will attract, and also a charged object will attract a neutral one.

Different objects made of different types of atoms and molecules will lose or gain electrons with different degrees of ease. If you rub a comb through your hair the comb will gain electrons from your hair. Remember this: it is a good base from which to start.

A Handful Of Static Electricity Experiments

THE STICKY BALLOON EXPERIMENT

You will have seen this at countless birthday parties. If you charge a balloon up by rubbing it on a jumper, then hold it near a neutral object, it will make the charges in that object move. If the neutral object is a conductor, then electrons will move easily to the other side, away from the balloon. If it is an insulator, the electrons in the atoms and molecules cannot move so far, but they will move slightly away. In either case, there will be more positive charges close to the negative balloon, and since opposites attract, the balloon will stick to the wall. Gradually the electrons will leak away and the balloon will gradually slide down the wall.

A HAIR-RAISING EXPERIMENT

Actually, you do this every time you comb your hair. You strip electrons off the hairs and cause each hair to be positively charged. Because they are all positively charged, they will repel one another. And if you have really combed your hair well and produced lots of charge, your hair will stand up. If you have difficulty with this, then try putting a bobble hat on and taking it off a few times. That should do it.

The bending stream of water

THE BENDING STREAM EXPERIMENT

This is similar to the bending candle flame experiment in Chapter Eleven. Charge your comb on your hair. Now turn on a tap so that you have a very thin stream of water. Bring the comb towards the water and you will see that it bends towards the comb.

AN EXPERIMENT WITH SALT AND PEPPER

This is always a good one to make a little money! At the dinner table get the salt cellar and the pepper pot and mix a little salt and pepper together. Challenge folk to separate the two as quickly as possible. You will probably find that someone suggests dissolving the salt. Fine, but that's messy. Far easier to get out your trusty comb – or if hygiene at the table precludes this, get a plastic pen and charge it on a sleeve, then hold it above the mixture. Abracadabra – you have separation.

MINI-LIGHTNING EXPERIMENTS

You will of course have noticed many occasions when you spark or get a shock. It is liable to happen when you are wearing a couple of layers of artificial fabrics, or when you get into a car and slide over nylon seat covering. You can also get it when reaching for a metal door handle after walking across a polyester rug. And you can occasionally get it when you kiss someone if one of you is really charged!

If you go into a darkened room with a roll of adhesive tape and quickly pull a strip off you may see a small blue flash. That is a discharge of static electricity, as are all the above sparks. And that is what lightning is, but on a much larger scale, of course.

You can create some visible mini-lightning bolts with a polystyrene plate and an aluminium metal pie dish. Firstly, fix a loop of sellotape to the pie dish so that you can pick it up without touching the metal. Next lay the polystyrene plate upside down on a table and rub it with a towel for a couple of minutes. This covers it in negative charge. Now gently drop the pie dish on top of it. If you now touch the metal you will get a small shock and perhaps see a spark. The spark will be easiest seen with the lights off. If you then lift the dish up by the loop and put your finger close again, you will get another spark. Place it down on the plate once more and yet again you will get another mini-bolt spark as you touch the metal.

I am sure that you now know precisely why this is happening. And it will go on happening until the static has gone.

Make Your Own Electroscope

An electroscope is a scientific instrument used to detect the presence and size of an electric charge on a body. Dr William Gilbert was the first person to experiment with this, using a simple instrument that he called a *versorium*. It was essentially a pivoting needle.

Any home experimenter worth his salt should have a go at making a simple electroscope.

REQUIREMENTS

✓ 1 small jar
✓ 2 strips of thin aluminium foil, 1cm x 5cm
✓ 1 paperclip
✓ piece of cardboard big enough to cover the mouth of the jar
✓ Sellotape

METHOD

Get hold of the middle part of the paperclip and bend it up so that you create an elongated figure 'S'. Hang the two strips of foil from the bottom hook and make a slit in the cardboard and thread the upper hook through it. Twist it round so that it will not fall through. Place the card over the

mouth of the jar so that the lower hook is inside the jar and the foil strips hang free. Tape the card to the jar so that it cannot move. If you wish you can surround the upper hook with a ball of foil.

Now simply bring various charged objects – after rubbing in your hair, or rubbing with wool or fur – close to the upper exposed hook. You will see that the foil strips separate, since they will both gain the same charge and will therefore repel one another. (If the source is negative then electrons will be pushed down the hook to the foil. If it is positive, electrons will be pulled up it from the foil.) The distance they move will be proportional to the size of the charge.

A home-made electroscope

BENJAMIN FRANKLIN AND HIS ELECTRIC KITE

Benjamin Franklin (1706–1790) was one of the Founding Fathers of America. He was a scientist, inventor, librarian and statesman. He invented countless things, including bifocal spectacles, swimming flippers and that saviour of innumerable buildings around the world ever since, the lightning rod.

He is mentioned here because of his famous lightning experiment. One night in 1752 he and his son were conducting experiments (no pun intended) during a thunderstorm. Ben was keen to prove that lightning was not a mysterious divine force, but electricity. He attached a metal spike to a kite and suspended a key from the kite. The kite was struck and the electrical discharge was conducted down the soaking wet string from the key, striking him and knocking him unconscious. He was extremely fortunate to survive. He proved by the experiment that lightning was electricity and that it flowed or could be conducted.

Hence the lightning rod invention.

BATTERIES

In 1791, Luigi Galvani (1737–1798), an anatomist and professor of obstetrics at Bologna University, was conducting experiments on 'animal electricity' when he discovered that the muscles of a dead frog twitched when a brass rod touched an iron plate upon which the frog had been laid out. He also noted that when other dead frogs were hung out to dry on a brass hook, the same twitching occurred if the brass hook happened to touch an iron fence. He concluded that electricity was at work, but he thought (incorrectly) that the twitching was caused by stored electrical charges in the frog muscles.

A colleague, Alessandro Volta (1745–1827), a professor of physics at Pavia University, disagreed. He felt that the muscle contractions were likely to be caused by an external stimulation, arising from the contact that was made between the iron and the brass.

Volta started experimenting with various metals to see if this effect could be reproduced. One of the things that he did was to use his tongue to detect anything that was happening. He found this to be a most effective method, for the tongue can detect very small electrical currents.

In 1799 he invented one of the most revolutionary aids to humankind – the Voltaic pile. This was made from stacking silver and zinc discs on top of each other, with a separating cardboard that had been soaked in brine between each unit of silver and zinc. This provided a continuous current of electricity, unlike the Leiden jars[18] that had been in use up until then.

Interestingly, the word 'battery' was coined by Benjamin Franklin in reference to an arrangement of Leiden jars, rather like a battery of cannons.

Make Your Own Voltaic Pile

And of course, this is a must-do experiment. You never know, one day you might have to get yourself out of a tricky situation by making electricity like this!

REQUIREMENTS

- ✓ 12 2p pieces
- ✓ silver (aluminium) foil
- ✓ blotting paper
- ✓ salt
- ✓ vinegar
- ✓ LED[19]
- ✓ insulating tape
- ✓ insulated copper wire – with bared ends

METHOD

Pour enough vinegar in a saucer to cover the bottom then dissolve as much salt as you can in it. This is to create an electrolyte. This is one of the essentials for any battery. Now cut discs the same size as the two pence pieces from the foil and the blotting paper.

Attach one end of wire to a disc of foil and one to a two pence piece. These will be your top and your bottom discs. The two pence will make the cathode or positive terminal and the foil will be the anode or negative terminal.

Soak the blotting paper in the electrolyte solution. Now start making

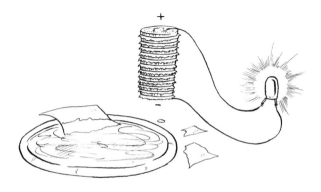

The arrangement for your Voltaic pile

And it really
works!

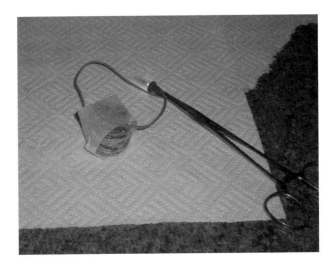

your pile. Put the foil disc with its attached wire on the bottom, then a
piece of blotting paper, then a two pence, then foil, then blotting paper,
then a two pence. Then keep going until you end with a two pence on the
top, with its attached wire. You have effectively made a series of cells. Now
simply attach your LED and watch it light up.

Explanation

All batteries need three components: an anode, a cathode and an electrolyte. All sorts of things can be used as electrolytes. Here we have used
salt and vinegar, but as you know from the above description, Volta just
used brine or sea water. You can use fruit juices, jam, or even just a potato!

There is potential energy in a battery. It converts chemical energy into
electrical energy. Inside the electrolyte negatively charged ions will migrate
towards the anode or negative pole. Each of the two pence and foil units
make up a cell, so effectively your pile is a number of cells in series.

When you form the circuit you get a flow of electricity so that you can
do fabulous things like light up LEDs. Back in 1812, Michael Faraday
made a Voltaic pile from seven old half pennies, seven discs of zinc and six
pieces of paper soaked in brine. With these he performed several experiments, including the decomposition of sulphate of magnesia.

Make Fruit And Potato Batteries

This is dead easy and quite fascinating. You will be surprised at how many
things you can make a working battery with. All you need are a couple of
screws or nails, one copper and one zinc. It helps to soften a fruit up a little
to get the electrolyte inside mobile. Then just insert the two screws or nails,

without them touching of course, and then attach them with wire to a bulb or LED.

If you care to try you can touch your tongue to the two terminals and you will feel a tiny current as a tickle. Well, it was good enough for Alessandro Volta.

MICHAEL FARADAY

We can go no further without a short consideration of one of the greatest scientists to study electricity. Michael Faraday (1791–1867) rose from humble beginnings, becoming assistant to Sir Humphry Davy at the Royal Institution before becoming a professor of chemistry and one of the most important scientists of all time. He is best known as the inventor of the dynamo, but he also discovered the laws of electrolysis, built several electric motors and discovered the chemical benzene. Appropriately, his name lives on in the name for an electrical unit (a Faraday is an amount of electricity measured during electrolysis).

ELECTROMAGNETISM

In 1820, Hans Christian Ørsted (1777–1851), a Danish physicist, discovered that a compass was deflected from its north–south orientation when a nearby battery was switched on. He deduced that an electric field from the electric current was thrown out in all directions. And that it was similar to a magnetic field.

This hugely important discovery was to lead to the development of the electric motor and the subsequent use of electricity as a power.

Make A Simple Electro-Magnet
This is so simple and so impressive.

REQUIREMENTS
✓ a 6-inch iron nail
✓ 3 feet of insulated copper wire
✓ a D cell battery

METHOD
Wrap the wire round the nail in a continuous, neat spiral. Leave a good six to eight inches at each end so that you can easily attach them to the battery. It is a good idea to incorporate a paper-clip switch, because you never want to operate it for long, since it will quickly heat up and it will swiftly drain the battery. The strength of the electromagnet depends upon the size of your battery and the number of coils you have made.

A simple
electromagnet

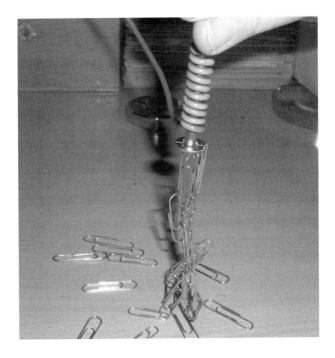

It does not matter which ends you connect to the battery, all that will change is the polarity of the electro-magnet. And it will only be magnetic as long as the electric circuit is on.

And there you go, experiment away with it: pick up paper clips or drawing pins. Why not get some iron filings and check out the electro-magnetic field that it throws out?

OHM'S LAW AND THE HISTORY IT TELLS

Electricity can be quite confusing, what with volts, amps and ohms. In fact these names all come from the scientists who helped shape our understanding of this amazing power upon which we depend so much these days.

The volt is, of course, named after Alessandro Volta. Voltage is effectively the power that propels a flow of electrons. It might help to think of a tank filled with water connected to a pipe that eventually leads to a water tap. The voltage would be like the difference in pressure of the water in the tank and the water that finally comes out of the tank. The difference between the two would be the potential voltage.

The amp is named after André Ampère (1775–1836), a French mathematician and physicist who carried out early research on electrical currents. In terms of the tank and pipe model, the current relates to the flow.

The ohm or unit of electrical resistance is named after Georg Simon Ohm (1787–1854), a German physicist who devised his law to show the relationship between voltage, current and resistance in electricity. In terms of our model, the resistance to the flow would be the size of the pipes and the size of the tap.

Mathematically, Ohm's law is formulated thus:

$$I \ = \ \frac{V}{R}$$

where **I** is current in amps, **V** is voltage in volts and **R** is resistance in ohms. Thus, if you know any two values for a circuit, you can calculate the third.

Make A Simple Electric Motor

I remember the first electric motor that I built. I was 11 and fancied that I was going to be a scientist one day. I have to admit that my first attempts with it were not hugely successful, and the design that I am going to give you might seem a bit Heath Robinson-ish, yet if you are patient it will

A simple electric motor

work. And you will get more of a kick from it than from just buying one or stripping one out of an old toy.

REQUIREMENTS

✓ a short piece of planking or balsa wood to act as a base
✓ 1 small cork
✓ 1 long needle
✓ horseshoe magnet with a gap of at least an inch
✓ 1 metre of insulated copper wire
✓ 4 nails
✓ 2 small panel pins
✓ 2 drawing pins
✓ a 9 volt battery

METHOD

Firstly, make the **armature** by inserting the needle through the cork, then placing the panel pins at an equal distance either side of the needle. Now bare the end of the wire and attach it to one pin. Now wrap the wire round and round the cork and bare its other end and attach it to the other pin.

Make the base by hammering in the nails as two crosses. These are to support the armature. Now use drawing pins to attach the bared ends of two wires, so that they will 'brush' the wires on the armature as it rotates. Attach the other ends to the battery, possibly incorporating a paperclip switch for ease.

Set the armature on the crossed nails and place your horseshoe magnet over it, fixing it on plasticene or gluing it if you want permanency.

You are all set to operate it. It may take a little help to start it spinning, but once it is off, you have a motor. And I leave it to you to devise uses for it.

Have fun!

CHAPTER FIFTEEN

BUILD YOUR OWN CRYSTAL SET RADIO

When I was growing up, the British comic industry was in full swing. Everybody had a weekly comic that they eagerly awaited to catch up on the latest instalment of their favourite serial character. At school you did swaps with your mates, and at night you read some of these cool adventures by torch under the blankets.

My own favourite was *The Hotspur*, published by DC Thomson of Dundee. One story I particularly liked was called Cat's Whiskers Kelly, the first instalment of which I am pleased to be able to show you here, courtesy of DC Thomson.

This story struck a chord with me, since my father had been in the Royal Signals during the Second World War and was working as a 'wireless operator'. It was inevitable, I suppose, that I should want to build my own working crystal set. And I did, although inevitably it disappeared many moons ago. Yet fear not, gentle reader, for one of the happy outcomes of this book is that I built another – and it works as well (or nearly as well, but perhaps my hearing is not quite as good as when I was a callow schoolboy!).

So have a read of Cat's Whiskers Kelly. Get into the mood, and then we'll talk a little about the early days of communications, crystal sets and cat whisker radios.

RADIO

We take so many things for granted these days. Yet when you think about it, radio is a fascinating phenomenon. To be able to tune into a whole host of different programmes from near or far is utterly amazing.

Guglielmo Marconi (1874–1937) was an Italian inventor, famed for his development of the radiotelegraph system. He made his first radio transmissions in 1896 and was joint winner of the 1909 Nobel Prize for Physics for his work on the system.

Radio is the transmission of signals by modulation of electromagnetic waves with frequencies below that of visible light. Radio waves can travel through air and even through the vacuum of space. In the early days it was called radio-telegraphy, which entered common parlance as wireless telegraphy, then simply as just 'wireless'. I must confess that when I was a kid it confused me as to why a radio was called a 'wireless set', since it contained a profusion of wires, dials and valves.

As I mentioned, my father was a 'wireless operator', so we always had old headphones, flex and valves littered about the house. There was certainly enough to make a crystal set.

Cat's whiskers radio, crystal set and Foxhole radio

All three of these names refer to a cheap powerless apparatus that can be used to pick up radio signals. If you have read the first episode of Cat's Whiskers Kelly from *The Hotspur* then you will see that his crystal set radio contained both a crystal and a cat's whisker. When he broke the crystal he inserted a piece of quartz, which just happened to allow him to pick up a particular agent working in France. But don't go away thinking that just any old crystal or bit of rock would do, or that some poor feline creature had been deprived of its natural antennae.

The crystal is in fact a diode, nothing more. If you are building your own then it is easy to buy one from your local electronics shop. But if you want to do it the old-fashioned way then you may want to use a crystal (usually of galena), or an old blue razor blade (or a hacksaw blade, which will be easier to find these days). The latter were used by American GIs serving in the Pacific during the Second World War. They called the sets they made Foxhole radios.

The cat's whisker is nothing more than a fine wire that contacts the crystal or diode. You will possibly find that a pencil stub works better and is a bit more robust. By moving it over the 'crystal' you find the most sensitive point.

The radio waves are received by an antenna, preferably a wire of 20 to 30 feet. A washing line is a possibility.

Never, ever use an antenna anywhere near live electricity, and always disconnect if there is a thunderstorm.

The antenna is attached to a tuned circuit to select the radio station. This tuned circuit consists of an induction coil. This also acts as a capacitor between its windings. A tuning slider will determine the number of windings of the coil that are used. This is the basis of tuning your radio.

A semiconductor detector, consisting of the crystal (diode) and the cat's

The two-page installment of Cat's Whiskers Kelly courtesy of DC Thomson

The rock that turned a wireless set into a war-winner.

NEXT WEEK—Action galore when the Black Bombers attack Britain!

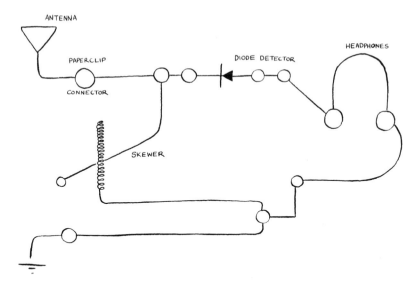

The circuit diagram for your crystal set

whisker (or substitute), extracts the signal from the radio carrier wave. It does this by only permitting the electrical signal to flow in one direction, so cutting out the hub-bub. This 'rectifies' the alternating current radio wave into a direct current pulse, which can then be picked up by the earpiece or earphones.

The set has to be grounded, and this can be directly to the ground, or via a cold water pipe.

Now Let's Build Your Crystal Set

Firstly, let's look at a circuit diagram. Don't be scared of this, it isn't complex. It is the plan that was used by GIs to build Foxhole razor blade radios during the Second World War.

REQUIREMENTS

✓ a toilet roll tube (or a firmer postal cylinder)
✓ a coil of enameled copper wire, about 75 feet
✓ a handful of paperclips
✓ a handful of drawing pins or panel pins (you can use wood screws instead of these if you want permanency. I would recommend this, actually)
✓ a board as a base
✓ a safety pin

✓ an old skewer or a metal tent peg
✓ a blue razor blade or blue hacksaw blade
✓ an earpiece or a set of old headphones (I got a pair cheaply on eBay!)
✓ a small pencil – just a couple of inches long with a sharp point. It is actually the pencil lead that you want

METHOD

Firstly, prepare your induction coil. This is a bit laborious, I warn you, but it has to be right. Make two small holes at each end of the tube about one centimetre from the edge. Firstly, secure the wire at the right hand of the tube by threading the wire through one hole and then back through the other, and back through the first again so that you can crimp it inside. Now, holding the tube in your left hand, start turning it in a direction away from you. As you do, use your right thumb to guide the coil wire. Keep doing this until you have done about a hundred turns. Put them close to each other, but don't overlap the loops. When you get to the left end cut the wire about ten inches from the last loop and then thread this through one hole and out the other. It is now ready to be fixed on the board with a couple of wood screws or tacks.

Using drawing pins attach the paperclips for the connections to the

My crystal set radio

And it sounds good!

antenna, the ground wire and the headphones (note that there are two clips for the headphones). Strip the enamel off the coil lead wire and attach it to the headphones' paperclip and then run it to the ground paper clip.

Get your skewer and with pliers bend it at an angle so that you will be able to secure it to the board by the hole and yet it will be able to rest on the coil, as in the photograph. This is the slider, which will allow you to tune in.

Now let's prepare the razor blade detector. Fix the razor blade or the hacksaw blade to the board with drawing pins and attach a wire from the antenna to the skewer-slider. Then attach a wire from the skewer-slider to the razor blade.

Take your safety pin and bend it at 90° at the head end, so that you can secure it to the board.

Take the pencil and very carefully remove the wood so that you just have the pencil lead. (If you are really lazy, just get a propelling pencil lead.) Now attach the sharpened pencil lead to the pointed end of the safety pin, letting it protrude beyond the safety pin tip by a quarter of an inch. Secure it with stripped wire, so that there is an excellent contact. Arrange it so that the pencil lead – your 'cat's whisker' – brushes the razor blade.

Now connect the safety pin to the second headphone connection.

Connect your headphones and you are almost there!

Get some sandpaper and strip the enamel off the coil where the slider is going to run across. This is important, of course. Adjust your slider so that it moves well.

The antenna needs about 30 feet of wire, preferably strung as high as possible. But again, note, don't have it anywhere near power sources. A washing line will work well.

To ground the set you can attach it to a metal cold water pipe. Obviously you may need to run long wires from the attachment paper clips, or arrange where you are going to install your crystal set radio.

Once you are all set up, to operate it you need to have the pencil lead just brushing the razor blade. Have a listen and experiment with the position of your slider. This is your tuner and you will eventually find the appropriate points to get the strongest signals from different radio stations.[20]

And that is it. Happy listening.

CHAPTER SIXTEEN

YOUR AMAZING BODY

When I was at school we seemed to have lots of lessons timetabled for 'gym', 'rugby', 'cricket' and stuff like that. Always followed by a cold shower. Amazing, the effect of cold showers on a male person's anatomy. I shall come back to that later on in the chapter, because I am sure that you will want to know why, now that I have whetted (wetted?) your interest.

Let's start with a little background to the fascinating history of anatomy. If you are squeamish, then just skip it and go to the first experiment.

FROM MUMMIES TO ANATOMY

Have you noticed the way that so many histories start with the ancient Egyptians? It is not surprising really, considering the great effort they took to preserve records about their lives when they built their tombs. Their written records have also been preserved in various papyri that have been unearthed by archaeologists over the last 200 or 300 years. For example, the Westcar Papyrus in the Berlin Museum tells tales of magic and conjuring performed at the court of King Khufu, the builder of the Great Pyramid. The Ebers Papyrus in the University of Leipzig Library, written about 1550BC, tells of Egyptian medical practices. The Edwin Smith Papyrus, now in the New York Academy of Medicine, written about the same time, outlines surgical techniques in those far-off days.

And of course, the ancient Egyptians practised mummification. You would have thought that this would have resulted in great knowledge about the body and the way that it functioned, because during the mummification process the embalmers removed the main organs and placed them in four canopic jars, which were traditionally guarded by four very fierce gods. Interestingly, the brain was not considered to be worthy of preservation and was extracted through the nose and discarded. The thing is that the purpose of mummification was to preserve the body for the afterlife, rather than to gain knowledge of its structure. Nevertheless, the Egyptians did record much useful information in their papyri.

The Greek physician Hippocrates of Cos (460–370BC) is credited as the Father of Medicine. He tried to introduce science to the practice of medicine, which at the time was still based on magic and superstition. He was certainly aware of many of the organs of the body and of the correct function of some of them. He discovered the tricuspid valve in the heart and wrote about it amid a whole series of books that are collectively known as the *Corpus Hippocraticum*. His name is forever associated with medicine, for he gave us the Hippocratic Oath, a modern variant of which is still said by all doctors when they qualify.

Aristotle (384–322BC) was a student of Plato and the first effective anatomist. He practised animal dissection and was the first to describe the difference between arteries and veins. The aorta, the great artery that leaves the heart, was named by him.

The great Library of Alexandria had been established in about 300BC and housed all of the great written works of Egyptian, Greek and Roman thinkers and natural philosophers. It was during the Ptolemaic period when Egypt was ruled by a succession of Roman rulers that further advances in anatomical knowledge were made. Drawing on the knowledge of the past, a Roman encyclopaedist, and possibly a doctor, Aulus Cornelius Celsus (25BC–AD50), wrote a great tome entitled *De Medicina* in which he detailed some of his anatomical findings. He wrote about the heart and the lungs, differentiated between the trachea (windpipe) and the oesophagus (gullet) and detailed the positions of the main organs.

In the second century the Greek physician Claudius Galenus of Pergamum (AD131–201), better known as Galen, performed several dissections on animals and accurately described many of the organs of the body. He described the function of the nerves and examined the structures of the eyes, ears, larynx and the reproductive organs. Writing in Latin, which has been the accepted language of anatomy ever since then, he named many structures of the body, including the *jejunum*,[21] part of the small bowel immediately after the duodenum; the *rectum*,[22] the lowest part of the large intestine, which terminates in the anus; and the *radius*,[23] one of the two forearm bones, on the thumb side.

Andreas Vesalius (1514–1564) was a Flemish anatomist who changed the very nature of medical education by bringing the students close to the operating table. He demonstrated that, in many instances, Galen and other early anatomists had been incorrect in some of their conclusions. For example, he demonstrated that the heart had four chambers. He conducted many human dissections and made many discoveries of far-reaching importance. Yet it was his writing that was to give him his place in medical history, thanks to the invention of the printing press. In 1543 he wrote the first anatomically accurate medical textbook, *De Humani Corporis Fabrica* (*On the Fabric of the Human Body*), which was complete with precise illustrations. In 1544 he was appointed court physician to the Emperor Charles V. From then until the emperor's abdication in 1556 Vesalius accompanied Charles on all his journeys and campaigns. Then he entered the service of King Philip II of Spain. In the spring of 1564 he undertook a pilgrimage to the Holy Land, from which he never returned.

Contemporary with Vesalius was the Italian anatomist and physician Bartolomeo Eustachi (1513–1574). He was the first to describe the teeth in detail, including their basic composition of enamel and dentine. He published the first accounts of the adrenal gland and thoracic duct as well as the first accurate description of the auditory tube, or pharyngotympanic tube, which was dubbed the 'Eustachian tube' in his honour. This tube links the middle ear to the throat.

Vesalius had two students who would push back the frontiers of anatomical knowledge considerably. First was Gabriele Falloppio (1523–1562), who studied under Vesalius in Padua. He discovered the Fallopian tubes, the trumpet-shaped tubes that collect and carry eggs from the ovaries to the uterus in females.

Fallopio in turn taught Girolamo Fabrizio (1537–1619), who became known to science as Fabricius. He is known as the Father of Embryology, for his studies on anatomy and the development of foetuses. To do the latter he studied their development in hen eggs. He also was the first person to describe the valves in veins. As we shall see, this was a fundamentally important discovery.

WILLIAM HARVEY AND THE CIRCULATION OF THE BLOOD

William Harvey (1578–1657) was a physician and anatomist who fought in the English Civil War and who was court physician to three kings of England. He had been personal physician to James I, then to Charles I. He went on campaign with King Charles I, and was in charge of the royal children's safety at the Battle of Edgehill. He is said to have hidden with them in a hedge and read a book to them. After the Restoration he became personal physician to King Charles II. After graduating from Cambridge University he went to Padua to study under Fabricius. After much research on animals he demonstrated the circulation of the blood and announced his discovery of the circulatory system in 1616. In 1628 he published his work *Exercitatio Anatomica de Motu Cordis et Sanguinis in Animalibus* (*An Anatomical Exercise on the Motion of the Heart and Blood in Animals*). It was the most significant piece of medical research ever written and laid the foundation for the scientific study of medicine.

Up until this point in time, although it was known that there was a difference between the blood in arteries and the blood in veins, it was thought that the heart manufactured arterial blood and that the liver manufactured venous blood, both types being sent to the to the extremities of the body by some sort of sucking mechanism of the heart and the liver. When the blood reached its target it was used up.

Harvey showed that this was not logical, since arithmetical calculation showed that a huge amount of blood would have to be produced and used up in a short period of time. He proposed that blood flowed through the heart in two separate loops, a pulmonary circulation going to the lungs and another, the systemic circulation, going to the organs and extremities.

His work under Fabricius helped him considerably, for he was aware of the valves in veins. Their function now became clear to him, for there was a reason why they only worked in one direction. Effectively, they were designed to allow blood to flow towards the heart, but not in the other direction. This suggested that the blood flowed around and around the body and that the two circulations were in some way linked. Although he was never able to show how the two loops met and exchanged the vital principle (which happens to be oxygen), he speculated that there was a means.

The experiment that he used to show this is very instructive and very simple, so we shall break off here, and you can try this yourself, with a helper.

The Circulation Of The Blood Experiment

That's right: this is a variant of *the* experiment that William Harvey used to demonstrate the circulation of the blood. If only you had been around in the mid-seventeenth century, you could have had the acclaim that William Harvey did. (If you could have worked out what was happening by yourself, that is!)

REQUIREMENTS

✓ an arm
✓ a helper

METHOD

Bare your helper's arm up to mid-biceps. Now grasp his or her arm above the elbow crease, as if you were about to feel the bulge of the biceps muscle. (Harvey used a tourniquet, but it is safer just to grip and the experiment still works). Maintain that grip. After a few moments you will find that the arm below your grip goes paler than the upper arm and that the veins in the lower arm start to stand out. A few moments later and the colour will start to go more purplish. If the veins are slow to stand out, then ask your helper to clench and unclench his or her fist. This will pump up the veins.

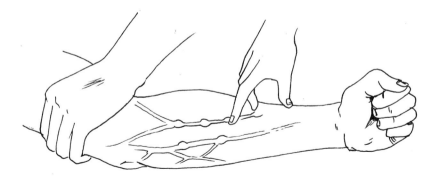

Harvey's experiment

Now look closely at a prominent vein (if your helper has got good veins that stand out) and you will see that every now and then there are little bumps. These are where there is a valve.

If you now with a finger stroke from one bulge up along the course of the vein to the next bulge, you will find that it empties and stays empty from that bump for a few moments. As soon as you lift your finger it will fill up. This is because you successfully emptied that section of vein between two valves. You cannot do it the other way.

Harvey tried this out with veins in other parts of the body, all with the same effect, apart from those in the neck. The neck veins only allowed blood to flow down, not upwards.

EXPLANATION

And this was Harvey's conclusion. The valves in the veins only permitted blood to flow towards the heart. He also concluded that the heart pumped blood around the circulation, through the two seemingly separate systems, the pulmonary and the systemic circulations.

You have just repeated his experiment.

Capillaries – the missing link

As I mentioned before the experiment, although Harvey speculated about there being a link between the arteries and the veins, he did not actually see this himself. This was because the necessary technology was not available to him.

Although an early microscope had been made in the Netherlands in about 1590, it was not adapted to medical or anatomical studies until the 1660s when Marcello Malpighi (1628–1694), an Italian doctor, began publishing his research. (See the chapter Under the Microscope). In an article about the anatomy of a frog's lung published in the journal of the Royal Society of England in 1661 he reported his findings on capillaries, the tiny blood vessels that link the arteries to the veins. His name is also remembered in the term 'the Malpighi layer', one of the deep living layers of the skin.

The blood supply to the brain

Another of King Charles I's physicians was Dr Thomas Willis (1621–1675) who with William Harvey fought on the royalist side during the English Civil War. Like Harvey he was an anatomist who was deeply interested in the blood supply of the body. He published several books in the 1660s, the most significant being a work about the brain. In it he described the circle of blood vessels at the base of the brain, formed from major arteries travelling up the front of the neck to join with ones from the back to produce an arterial circle, which gave off branches to supply blood to the various areas of the brain. This is called the Circle of Willis.

John Hunter

I want to finish this potted history of anatomy with John Hunter (1728–1793), one of the most distinguished surgeons and anatomists of his day. He was born in East Kilbride in Lanarkshire, Scotland, the youngest of 10 children. His brother William ran a school of anatomy in London. At the age of 21 John went to visit him, with the intention of joining the army. However, they discovered that he had an aptitude for dissection, and he stayed on as William's assistant. His skills were soon to eclipse those of his brother and he went on to become one of the most famous surgeons of his time.

Hunter's anatomical discoveries helped to advance surgery significantly. He discovered the function of the lymphatic system, unravelled many of the mysteries of digestion and made an extensive study of teeth. He was the first to explain the development of the child, and he wrote extensively on inflammation, gunshot wounds, and venereal disease.

John Hunter gathered many honours in his career and became personal surgeon to King George III. He also opened his own school of anatomy and began to assemble a medical and anatomical museum with over 14,000 preparations of over 500 species of plant and animals, including many human dissection studies. Many of these specimens can be seen at the Hunter Museum, which is housed at the Royal College of Surgeons in London.

Make A Simple Pulseometer

The pulse reflects the heartbeat. Every time your heart beats it send out a pulse of pressure, which travels through the arteries of your body. When a doctor feels your pulse he or she is checking that impulse and assessing the rate of the heart, the rhythm of the heartbeat and the strength of the pulse. It is obviously beyond the scope of this book to teach you how to examine a pulse properly. But I can tell you what to do to feel your pulse, and with a little gadget, you can see it.

You can feel the pulse over any of the arteries of the body. In a full medical examination a doctor will feel the *carotid arteries* in the neck, the *radial arteries* at the wrists, the *femoral arteries* in the groins, the *posterior popliteals* behind the knee, the *posterior tibials* behind the inner ankle bone and the *dorsalis pedi* on top of the foot. If you feel the pulse over any two at the same time, you should feel the same pulse.

For most purposes you just need to feel the radial pulse at the wrist. You will find it as in the illustration, on the thumb side of the wrist.

To make a pulsometer just take a drawing pin and slip a match over the point. Then with the wrist flat on a table, place it over the radial pulse. You will then 'see' your own pulse. You can time I how many beats it gives over a minute to give you the heart rate.

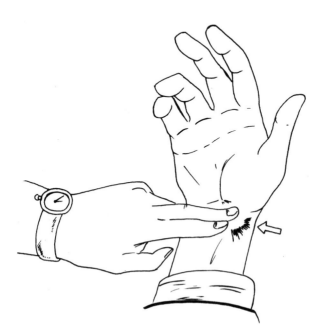

Taking the radial
pulse

A simple
pulsometer

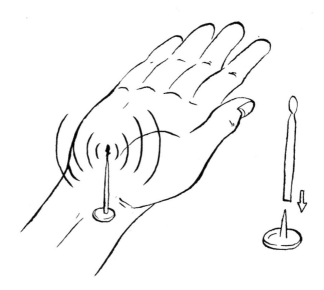

A Pulse-Stopping Experiment

As you know, as long as you can feel a pulse, you know that the individual is alive! It is said that eastern adepts are able to control their pulse just by thought, and can even stop it. Does that sound possible?

No? Well, try this experiment.

REQUIREMENT

✓ a rolled up pair of socks, or a golf ball

METHOD

Place the ball under your clothes under the armpit (we call this the axilla) on the same side that you are proposing to have your pulse taken. Allow someone to take your pulse. Then inform him or her that with some concentration you can slow this down and even stop it.

You simply press your arm against your side. If your pulse is then taken, it will not be felt. But you can, of course, allow it to restart at will!

A pulse-stopping experiment

The axillary artery, the main supply to the arm, passes through the axilla. You have compressed it slightly with the ball to prevent the pulse being felt. Do not do it for too long or you will get a pins and needles feeling in the arm and hand.

THOSE AMAZING MUSCLES

There are over 650 muscles in the body and they are of 3 types – skeletal, cardiac (heart) and smooth (visceral) muscles. The skeletal muscles are arranged in groups around the joints, their function being to move the joints. They account for between 40 and 50 per cent of the body's weight.

Most muscles have a similar structure, consisting of a fleshy contractile part known as the muscle belly, and a point of origin and a point of insertion. The point of origin is where the muscle is anchored to bone. The point of insertion is where it is attached to the bone that it has the job of moving.

Muscles are arranged in opposing pairs. Each muscle is only capable of pulling in one direction. The muscle it is paired with pulls in the opposite direction. When a muscle belly contracts it pulls the bone at the point of insertion towards it. At the same time the opposing muscle of the pair will relax. This is easiest understood by thinking of the biceps and the triceps muscles in the arm. When the biceps contracts it pulls the arm up towards the shoulder. When the triceps contracts it pulls in the opposite direction to straighten the arm.

The Roman finger test

Take These Muscle Memory Tests
That's right, I said muscle memory! You may not think it, but your body retains a muscle memory. Just try these three tests.

ROMAN FINGER TEST
Try this one yourself and then have a go with your family. Best to do it one at a time, though. It has a bigger impact that way.

Place your hand, it doesn't matter which one, on a flat table surface. Bend your middle finger underneath with the knuckle resting on the table, but keep all the other fingers and the thumb straight out on the table.

Now lift your forefinger – no problem. Put it back again. Now lift your thumb – a doddle. Put it back and lift the little finger - so simple. OK, so put it back and now lift the fourth or the ring finger – wow!

You can't do it. That is interesting.

THE HYPNOTIZED FINGER TEST

This time you are going to hypnotize yourself. That's right, hypnotize yourself. Clasp your hands together, except for the forefingers. Make a steeple with them. Now imagine that you have a rubber band wound around them, so tight that it doesn't want you to separate them.

Ok, so now you separate them about an inch apart at the tips. But because you have 'hypnotized' your- self about the rubber band, you will see that in a second or two, they feel that they just have to close again.

There you go!

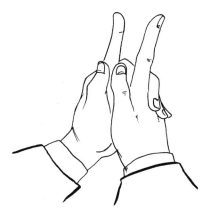

The hypnotized finger test

THE DOORWAY MUSCLE TEST AND EXPLANATION

Stand inside a doorway with your arms hanging by your sides. Now reach out and press the backs of your hands against the inside of the door frame. Push as hard as you can for 30 seconds. Then step forward out of the doorway, letting your arms hang loosely by your sides. Now just move your arms a little bit. You will find that they will feel as if they are moving upwards of their own accord.

Roughly speaking, this is muscle memory. We depend a lot on muscle memory, although in a sense it is a bit of a misnomer. The muscles them- selves do not have a memory, but the nervous and muscular system interact in such a way that the brain is able to determine where our limbs are in space and how much tension there is in them. Through repetitions we learn how to make fine precise movements and large powerful movements. We refer to these as motor skills.

There are two types of motor skills. Fine motor refers to the precise movements, the fine skills such as we use in picking up little objects, combing hair or brushing teeth. Gross motor refers to moving the big muscles in lifting, digging, throwing, or any of the major sporting activities.

When you watch a baby learn how to crawl, then develop into a toddler, you are seeing this amazing ability of the body to adapt. The child is developing muscle memory so that the walking becomes more balanced, more adept, until it is eventually a completely natural process.

And the same thing happens as we develop skills, as in learning a new sport, or learning how to play a musical instrument. A golf swing, a tennis serve, playing the chords on a guitar, are all examples. You build up a complex muscle memory of the movements until it becomes second nature.

In the tests you just did, muscle memory was involved to an extent. The first test is a bit of a cheat. You have simply put your body into a position where it is mechanically very difficult to make that movement. In the second test your flexor muscles, which close your hand, overpower the extensor muscles, which want to keep it open. And in the third, you have stimulated the muscles to move and they will tend to continue the movement even after you have stopped. That is what we loosely mean by muscle memory.

Not everybody has the same muscles

You would think that everybody has exactly the same muscle structure, wouldn't you? Well, by and large we do, yet there are sometimes subtle differences. As I already mentioned, in anatomy we describe each muscle as having an origin and an insertion. Its origin is the bone that it is anchored to, and its insertion is to the bones or structure that it has the function of moving. Both the origin and the insertion can vary slightly in individuals. That slight change in position may affect the function very slightly. That change may be an advantage or a disadvantage.

In addition to these subtle differences, there are in fact muscles that are 'coming' or 'going'. This is utterly fascinating, since they represent an element of proof about the great Charles Darwin's Theory of Evolution, because these 'coming and going' muscles represent muscles that are appearing in a species or ones that are disappearing.

The *Palmaris Longus* is a muscle that can be made to stand out at the wrist by flexing your palm towards the forearm. It will be apparent as a cord-like tendon. It is absent in about 15 per cent of the population. Not having one does not affect the strength of the wrist or the hand. It is a muscle that is used in other species to expose the claws! We don't do that any longer, so it is a gradually disappearing muscle.

The *Peroneus Tertius* muscle in the foot is an appearing muscle. It is absent in just over six per cent of the population. It seems to be an appearing muscle in the species. It gives the foot additional mobility and may be helpful in runners or dancers.

Vestigiality

This refers to structures or organs that no longer have a function in a species. They are another indication of the evolution of a species. And we humans have several of these.

Let us start at the top of the body and work down. Firstly, there is the *Occipito-frontalis* muscle. In many species this muscle extends from the back of the head (the occiput) to the forehead (the frontal bone). In many animals it helps to keep the head from falling. In humans it has become a sheet-like structure called an aponeurosis that forms part of the scalp. It no longer holds the head up, since we are erect creatures, but it helps to raise the eyebrows and crease the forehead in facial expression.

If you look at the inner corner of the eye (the nasal side), you will see a small pink membrane. This is called the *plica semilunaris*, which is actually a fold of the conjunctiva. It is a vestige of the nictitating membrane, or the third eyelid, that can still be seen in sharks, many reptiles, birds, camels and polar bears.

Look at the ear. Can you make it move? Some people can, but many can't. It depends on whether you have active muscles to move it. You may be able to train those muscles. At one time humans would have been able to move their ears and they would have had pointed ears like other simians, which would have flapped over, like those of a monkey, dog or a cat. A vestige of the ear flap is shown in the accompanying drawing. Charles Darwin discusses this in his second important book, *The Descent of Man*, published in 1871. In anatomy this is known as Darwin's Tubercle.

The *Platysma* muscle is a broad sheet of muscle on each side of the neck, extending from the upper part of the shoulder to the corner of the mouth, the action of which wrinkles the skin of the neck and depresses the corner of the mouth. This in fact is a vestigial remnant of the *panniculus carnosus*

Darwin's tubercle is a vestige of our pointed ear!

of animals that shake their skins. You can best see it in horses, when they flick flies off their backs.

The appendix in the bowel is huge in animals like rabbits, but little more than a small sac in humans. Similarly, the coccyx or tail bones are no longer external, but exist as an internal tail.

Finally, whenever you get goosebumps, you are experiencing the effect of a vestigial reflex. It is designed to make fur or hair stand on end, to make you look bigger, or to trap air in the hair to retain heat. Fascinating, is it not?

DOCTORS' EXAMINATIONS

Since we started talking about pulses we might as well consider a little more about the sort of things that doctors do when they examine you in order to diagnose a complaint. Essentially, there are four mainstays of examination. These are inspection, palpation, percussion and auscultation.

Inspection means that you look and try to make deductions according to the overall appearance of the patient and the presence of any particular features.

Palpation means feeling to see whether there are any abnormalities. Feeling the pulse is part of this process.

Percussion is an interesting process, which involves tapping on the body to see if you can feel any unusual vibrations, and hear alterations in the notes that you produce when you tap over a finger.

Auscultation is the process of listening to the internal workings of the body, usually with a stethoscope.

From wine barrels to chests

I was examining a gentleman's chest one day and was surprised when he suddenly went into a fit of laughter.

'My chest sounds just like an old barrel,' he explained. Then he asked me why doctors always tapped on his chest before they listened with their stethoscope.

So I told him that it was to get an idea of the state of the inner organs. He was delighted when I told him that he had actually been correct when he used the barrel analogy, because it was from tapping wine casks that the technique was devised. Or so the story goes.

When anatomy and physiology started to give doctors an idea of what really happened in the body (a taste of which I have tried to give you in this chapter), there was a need to be able to work out the state of the internal organs. Towards the end of the eighteenth century an Austrian physician, Dr Leopold Auenbrugger (1722–1809), made the break-through when he invented the simple technique of percussion.

Leopold von Auenbrugger's father was a hotel owner. It is thought that the method used to check on the level of wine in casks, by tapping on them to determine where the level of wine was, was something that he had seen in his father's cellar throughout his child-hood. His genius was in adapting it to the human body. The technique involves laying one hand flat on the part of the body to be examined, usually the chest or the abdomen.

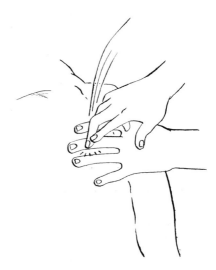

Percussing someone's chest

The middle finger of one hand then taps the middle bone of the middle finger of the flattened hand in order to produce a noise. Four types of noise can thus be elicited, allowing the examiner to determine the state of certain organs. Essentially, the amount of dullness or hollowness can give a lot of information, and it can help in determining whether or not fluid is present.

Von Auenbrugger spent 10 years examining thousands of patients and correlating post-mortem findings in order to build up a whole science of percussion. He developed the pleximeter, a piece of ivory, bone or wood,

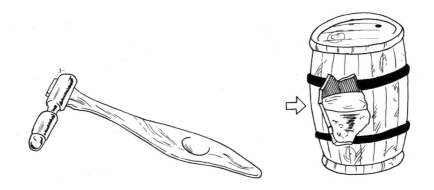

Auenbrugger developed his pleximeter method from seeing his father tapping barrels

which was held over the part of the body to be examined, which was then lightly tapped with a special small hammer to produce a resonant note.

His book, *Inventum Novum*, first published in 1851 then translated into English as *A New Discovery that Enables the Physician from the Percussion of the Human Thorax to Detect the Diseases Hidden Within the Chest*, is now considered one of the most important classics of medicine. And it all started with those wine casks in his father's cellar.

From a rolled-up piece of paper to the doctor's badge of office

You always associate a doctor with a stethoscope, don't you? Well, until the nineteenth century, you would be more likely to associate him with a urine bottle. You see, uroscopy, or making a diagnosis according to the appearance *and taste* of the patient's urine, was the main thing expected of a doctor. Percussion had changed that slightly, but a bigger change was to come thanks to the French physician René Théophile Hyacinthe Laennec (1781–1826), when he invented the stethoscope in 1816.

He had been influenced by Dr Auenbrugger's percussion method and was intrigued by the possibility of listening to body sounds. His first experiment with this was during a consultation with a young female

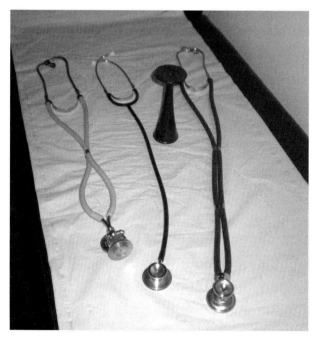

Various types of stethoscope

patient, whom he suspected of having a heart condition. He simply rolled up a piece of stiff paper into a cylinder and listened down it to the lady's heart. He was amazed by the way it magnified the sound of the heart so that he could imagine what was happening.

Over the years he refined his instrument, creating a long wooden tube with a funnel for collecting the sounds. A form of this instrument is still used by doctors today when they are listening for the sound of a baby's heart in a pregnant lady.

The modern two-ear type of stethoscope that you associate with doctors nowadays was invented in 1852 by the American physician Dr George Cammann. It has changed very little since then.

Reflexes

I am sure you will have seen a doctor testing reflexes with a small tendon hammer. A reflex is basically an action that is directed backwards. It comes from the Latin *reflexus*, meaning 'go back'.

There are many reflexes in the body, both of the muscles and of the inner organs. The **knee jerk reflex** occurs when the patellar tendon at the knee is struck, since a loop causes the quadriceps muscle to contract. The **gastro-colic reflex** occurs whenever food enters the stomach, causing the lower bowel, the colon to start making room and moving its contents further down. And artificial conditioned reflexes can occur, as were proven by Ivan Pavlov and his salivating Alsatian dog.

Here are a few interesting ones.

Pupillary reflexes   The pupil is the so-called apple of the eye, which was called by the Roman's the 'little doll' – from the Latin *papilla*, meaning

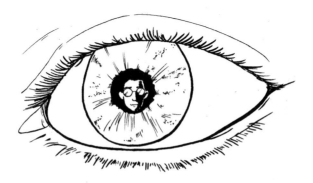

The pupil of the
eye

small doll. The reason for this is that a small person like a tiny doll (a reflection) is seen in the pupil of the eye.

The pupil responds to light and to accommodation. This means that if you shine a light in the eye or look into a light the pupil will reflexly shrink in size, to limit the amount of light allowed in the eye. On the other hand, if you cover the eye momentarily, or if you go into shade, the pupil will open as much as it can to let the maximum amount of light in.

If you look at someone's pupil as he or she looks at something close at hand or something in the distance, the pupils will accommodate for the different distances.

There is an interesting additional reflex that you can test on yourself. It is called the **ciliospinal reflex**. If you look at your eye in a mirror and then pinch the skin of your neck, face or trunk you will momentarily see a change in the pupil size. It will get bigger.

Cremasteric reflex   The cremaster muscle is only found in males. It covers the testicles and its purpose is to raise or lower the testicles. This is because the testicles function at a lower temperature than the inside of the body, which is why they are outside it, contained in the sac called the scrotum. When it is cold the cremaster muscle contracts to bring the scrotum and the testicles closer to the abdomen, and when it is warm, it relaxes to allow them to sink into the scrotum and become cool.

The cremastric reflex stimulates the cremaster to function. This can be tested in the bath. If the skin of the inner thigh is gently stroked downwards, from the direction of the hip towards the knee, the cremaster on the same side will operate to lift the testicle on that side.

And you will remember that I started this chapter with a memory of school games day and the effect of cold showers. Well, now you know why that happens.

30 THINGS YOU MIGHT NOT HAVE KNOWN ABOUT THE BODY

1. The adult human body is made up of about 50 to 75 trillion cells
2. All of the functioning cells in the body will be replaced over about a 10-year period
3. The average stomach lining cell is replaced every 5 days, your red blood cells live for 120 days, your liver cells are replaced every 18 months and your bone cells are replaced every 10 years
4. 15 billion blood cells are destroyed and the same number are produced every second
5. Only 10 per cent of the total body mass is made up of human cells, the rest are microbes
6. The brain is made up of about 100 billion cells
7. The average taste bud lives for 10 days

8. 80 per cent of the human body is made up of water
9. Nerve impulses to and from the brain travel at speeds of up to 170 miles an hour
10. The average human heart will beat 3,000 million times in its lifetime and pump 48 million gallons of blood
11. The adult intestine is about 25 feet long
12. Cartilage (which lines joints) is eight times slippier than ice
13. The teeth are the only place in the body where bone naturally comes through skin
14. At the age of 6 most people have 48 teeth in their head (20 baby teeth and most of the developing 32 adult teeth)
15. Tooth enamel is the hardest tissue of any animal or plant.
16. When you are born you have over 300 assorted bones
17. By adulthood many bones will have fused to leave 206
18. The healthy human thigh bone is stronger than concrete
19. Babies do not have knee-caps. The patella is a sesamoid bone, which means it develops inside a tendon. It only develops at about the age of two
20. The average human head weights eight pounds
21. The average human scalp has 100,000 hairs (even bald people, whose hairs are very thin, short and fine)
22. It takes 72 different muscles to produce speech
23. Humans have internal tails
24. Your fingerprints are unique to you
25. The acid in your stomach could eat through wood
26. Human ears may once have been pointed, like a dog's. Charles Darwin, the scientist who discovered the Theory of Evolution, suggested this, and a vestigial flap on the ear is still called Darwin's tubercle
27. The view of the world is slightly different in each eye, thereby allowing you to perceive depth
28. Your ears hear at different times, thereby allowing you to pinpoint the source of sounds
29. Your two nostrils pick up different types of smells
30. You use 30 muscles to smile

CHAPTER SEVENTEEN

THOSE INCREDIBLE SENSES
... AND HOW TO FOOL THEM

Every schoolboy and schoolgirl knows that you have five senses. They are sight, hearing, touch, smell and taste. They are all really quite incredible and quite necessary for us to interpret the world about us. Understandably, they can sometimes be fooled – and that can be quite fun.

SIGHT

The eye is the organ that enables us to see. When I was studying biology at school we each received a bull's eye to dissect. That no longer happens, which in some ways I feel is a shame, because handling the tissues gave you a respect for the wonder of nature. On the other hand it was rather messy and I do recall that a couple of chaps in the class felt queasy and were duly sent to the sick room.

In fact, the following little diagram of a section through the eye will give you all the information that you need for now, without dissecting anything.

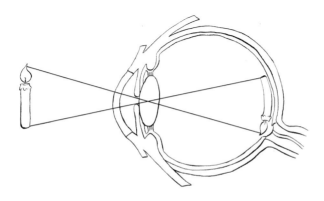

The anatomy of the eye

The chain of perception

There are three links in the chain of events that result in sight. The first is external and involves light illuminating an object and light waves reaching the eye. The second is the physical visual apparatus, from eye to brain, consisting of nervous pathways leading to the part of the brain that starts the processing of information. Finally, the third and most complex is the interpretation of the visual stimulus and the creation of the internal model of the world that is used by the consciousness.

As you can see in the diagram, the eye is basically a spherical camera. The muscular **sclera**, or the white of the eye, forms the sphere and is continuous with the transparent front of the eye, the **cornea**. Light rays enter the eye and are focused by the **lens** on to the **retina**, which is the light-sensitive 'seeing' membrane at the back of the eye. The amount of light let into the eye is determined by the reflex actions that govern the movement of the **iris**, and the shape of the lens and the focus is adjusted by the **ciliary muscles**. There are two fluids in the eye, the **aqueous humor** at the front of the eye and the jelly-like **vitreous humor** behind the lens.

The retina has two types of cells, called **rods** and **cones**. There are about 120 million rods in the eye and about 6 to 7 million cones, which are colour sensitive. The rods are distributed about the whole retina, but the cones are predominantly situated around the centre of the eye, the part called the **macula**.

Signals from the eye are transmitted back to the brain via the optic nerve, which is the second of the 12 cranial nerves.[24] Now it gets a bit complicated and really quite interesting. This is because the part of the brain that actually perceives what you see is in the back of the brain! Don't you think that is odd? Well, it gets odder!

Take a look at the next diagram, which shows the optic pathway. This is the route by which nerve impulses from the eyes are passed to the back of the brain. You will note that each eye is shown as having a full line and a dotted line passing from the eye into the brain. The full line represents the nerve impulses that are transmitted

The optic pathways

from the left half of each eye. The dotted line represents the nerve impulses that are transmitted from the right half of each eye. Note that the light rays coming into the eye have crossed. They would also have crossed from top to bottom, so that the image formed in the camera of the eye is upside down and turned around.

Follow the lines and you will see that the two nerve impulses from the inner half of each eye cross over at a point called the **optic chiasma**. They then pass back to the **visual cortex** at the back of the brain as the **optic radiation**. The visual cortex then does an amazing thing. It turns the image formed by the camera the right way up and orientates it so that you see the world as it is.

Optical illusions

Generally the brain and the mind are extremely good at matching up the image that is built up with past images it has retained from past experience. Sometimes, however, the visual stimulus and the retained memory do not match, but the mind patches over the two to perceive what 'seems' to be there. This effectively is an optical illusion. An optical illusion can arise in any of the three links of visual perception.

First link illusions   A **mirage** is an example of an external illusion, created in the first, physical link involving what happens to the light rays before they reach the eye. This is due to refraction or bending of those rays by alternate layers of hot and cool air. Often it will create the illusion of water, accompanied by inverted reflections of distant objects.

CASTLES IN THE SKY

Well, not exactly castles, but a town in the sky. The Fata Morgana is a type of mirage that was first described in the early nineteenth century in the Straits of Messina, between Sicily and Italy. Under the right conditions, a whole town can be seen in the sky. It is thought to be a mirage of a fishing village situated further along the coast.

So too is the **flying saucer effect**. Just put the tips of your fingers together and hold them three inches in front of your eyes. Now gradually draw them apart and you will see the 'flying saucer' floating between the ends of your fingers. This occurs because you are allowing yourself to go cross-eyed to produce the illusion.

Second link illusions   When we stare at a brightly illuminated red disk for a time, then transfer our attention to a white paper, we see a green disk. The green disk is an illusion created in the second, physiological link. It is an afterimage.

The **bendy pencil illusion** is another example of this as well as perception, due to the speed at which a movement takes place. Just get hold of a pencil by its blunt end and waggle it up and down with a floppy wrist. You will create the illusion that it is bending like rubber.

The phantom coin is yet another example. Hold two coins together by the forefinger of each hand and rub them up and down. You will create the illusion that there is a third coin caught between the other two. It always looks as if it is lower than the two coins.

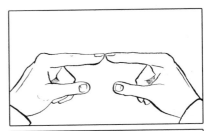

And finally, the **missing digit trick** makes it look as if you have lost the last two phalanges of your second finger. This requires practice, but will reward you with an instant optical illusion to fool people with.

There are two moves you have to practise in front of a mirror until they are second nature. Look at the diagram to see. Firstly, there is the scissors position and secondly there is the bent second finger position. Basically you spin the hand round,

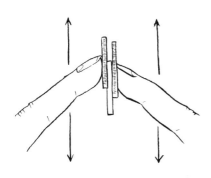

The phantom coin always seems to be lower than the others

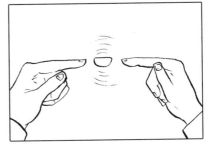

The flying saucer illusion

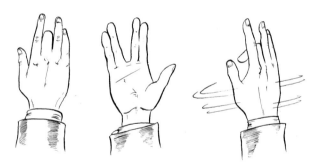

The missing digit

back and forth several times, changing from one position to the other. The bent second finger position is the one that is shown to the audience and then the spinning back and forth goes on to produce the effect.

Third link illusions   For an example of a third link illusion, let's do an experiment.

The Harvest Moon Experiment

For centuries we have studied the moon and been aware that at certain times the full moon, when it is close to the horizon, appears huge. Various explanations have been given over the millennia, ranging from the mystical to more modern explanations such as refraction and the bending of light. Now you can perform a simple experiment to see if there isn't a simpler explanation.

REQUIREMENTS

✓ a clear evening
✓ a full (or Harvest) moon, lying near the horizon

METHOD

This is actually a very simple experiment. Next time that you see a low-lying moon, the chances are that it will seem huge, possibly two or three times as big as usual, to you and everyone around you.

Focus on the horizon full moon for a few moments then slowly raise your hand to cover the horizon. Then blink and look at the moon again. It should return to its true perceived size. Blink again and remove the hand and it will again be perceived as large.

You will gather that your hand is not likely to have cut out any mystical force or have stopped the bending of light beams. What you have seen is simply a trick of the mind.

EXPLANATION

This is all about the chain of perception that I mentioned earlier. This is an illusion arising from the third link within the part of the brain that creates the imagery and links it to the retained memory. The retained memory tells us that when things appear close to the horizon they are nearer and larger than they are high up in the sky. When the moon is low, we 'mis-perceive' the moon to be larger than it is.

The Harvest Moon illusion

It is as simple as that.

SMELL AND TASTE

Taste and smell are the two 'chemical' senses, in that they depend upon their receptors being stimulated by chemical molecules, rather than by energy from light, pressure, or sound. Of the two senses, smell is more sensitive, since as little as one molecule in a million may be detected by the nose, but it takes a minimum of one part per thousand to stimulate the tongue. The olfactory nerve, which transmits smell, is the first cranial nerve.

The sense of smell is extremely important and in days gone by was valuable for locating food, warning of danger and contributing to attraction to other people. Of all the senses, it is unique, in that the scent message passes directly through the limbic system, the emotional centre of the brain. Hence we often react instantly and instinctively to different smells as they either please or displease us.

Taste is also important to us. After all, it drives appetite and it protects us from poisons. Thus we like the taste of sugar because we have need of carbohydrates. We get cravings for salt because we must have sodium chloride or salt in our diet. Bitter and sour tastes cause unpleasant feelings and even avoidance reactions because most poisons are bitter. And when food goes off it goes sour or acidic. You might ponder the question, why do medicines all taste bitter? Because they are, in fact, potentially poisonous when too much is taken.

Finally, we have an absolute need for protein, and amino acids are the building blocks for proteins, so the more recently described taste quality **umami** (pronounced 'oo-marmie'), which is the meaty, savoury taste, drives our appetite for amino acids. This taste has been known to the

Japanese for a long time but has only recently been recognized by the west. Bacon, soy sauce and monosodium glutamate all strongly stimulate our umami receptors. Indeed, bacon is a rich source of amino acids. Taste is stimulated through our taste buds, of which the average tongue has about 9,000.

When we perceive a flavour, we are probably using 75 per cent smell and 25 per cent taste. Don't believe me? Then try this little tasting experiment

The Nose Pinch Experiment
You can tell the difference between tea and coffee, or between grated apple and grated onion, can't you?

REQUIREMENTS
✓ a blindfold
✓ a helper
✓ a cup of coffee, a cup of tea; a grated apple, a grated onion; a piece of grated cheese and a piece of grated chocolate; any other strange-tasting pairs of food – but prepare them in a similar way so that no clues are given by texture. Take care with the drinks and don't have them too hot if you are using the blindfold.

METHOD
Arrange the paired foods on saucers. Get your helper to blindfold you and then get him or her to mix the plates up. You then hold your nose throughout the experiment. He or she should tell you which pairing is being tested and a spoon of one is placed in the mouth. Then the other one is tasted and you then say which is which.

It is also worth repeating the test after you have used some tissue paper to dry your tongue before testing.

EXPLANATION
You may have found that quite interesting and quite revealing. When you deprive yourself of smell you are reducing your tasting ability to a quarter. And when you dry the tongue you are depriving the food of the benefit of saliva to dissolve in, so it will take a while for the flavour to be apparent. But even then the flavours may seem quite distorted.

The Salt And Flour Experiment
Did you know that you can make salt taste like sugar? Try this little experiment and see.

✓ a pinch of salt and a pinch of flour

METHOD
Put a tiny pinch of salt on a plate. Then just gather a few grains and pop them on your tongue. You will of course recognize the taste of salt. Now get a pinch of flour and mix it with the salt on the plate. Now put a little on your tongue and wait a few seconds. The saltiness will disappear and instead you will taste the sweetness of sugar.

EXPLANATION
Well, it is a bit of a trick. You haven't really made the salt taste like sugar, but you have made the flour change. What happens is that the few salt grains dissolve in your saliva. At the same time an enzyme called **ptyalin** in your saliva starts to break the flour down into sugar and so you taste the sweetness.

HEARING

The human ear is the organ of hearing. We tend to think about it having three parts. The outer ear consists of the **pinna** (also called the auricle) and the **ear canal**. The function of this is to collect sound waves and direct them down the canal towards the ear drum. You instinctively enhance the effect of the pinna when you cup an ear to hear better.

The middle ear consists of the **ear drum**, the three little **ossicle** bones

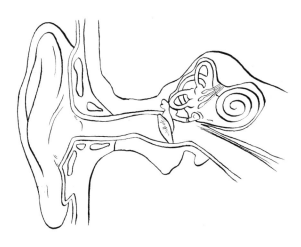

The anatomy of
the ear

(**malleus, incus** and **stapes**; respectively hammer, anvil and stirrup, after their shapes) and the **Eustachian tube**, which links this chamber with the back of the throat. The Eustachian tube has the function of equalizing the pressure in the middle ear with the outside atmosphere. This is why your ears pop when you change altitude; you swallow and the Eustachian tube opens and the pressure is balanced. Sometimes when the pressure is great you have to hold your nose and try to blow to open the tube to make the ears pop to ease the discomfort. The function of the middle ear is to transmit the vibrations on the ear drum through the ossicles to vibrate the **oval window** of the inner ear. They amplify the sound, effectively.

The inner ear consists of the bony labyrinth. It has two parts – the **cochlea**, or the organ of hearing, which is shaped like a snail's shell, and the **semi-circular canals**, which help us to balance. The acoustic nerve is the eighth cranial nerve. It relays information about hearing from the cochlea and about balance from the semi-circular canals to the brain.

Is that really the sea I hear?

When you were little, did you ever listen to the sound of the crashing waves in a sea shell? I bet you did, and I expect you were filled with wonder at it. Of course, you are not really hearing the sea. This is nothing but ambient noise that you are amplifying by holding the shell near your ear. You don't actually need a shell, since a mug or a cup will do the same.

Maybe that is where the expression 'storm in a tea cup' comes from?

Sound effects

Of course, radio would be lost without the sound effects department. They can create the most amazing perceptions of sound from very different stimuli. You might try these on your friends and family (while they close their eyes and imagine):

- crackle cellophane to give the sound of a fire
- flap a pair of gloves to mimic a bird flying
- fill a tin with stones, a few bits of metal and pieces of glass (careful!), seal with tape. Roll it on the ground to produce a crash!
- shake a Perspex sheet for thunder
- and, of course, don't forget the famous coconut shells filled with wadding to simulate a horse

The thing is, the brain perceives the sound when it is delivered in the right context.

The neck cracking illusion   This is a neat practical joke that has a high cringe factor, if people are not expecting it. You secretly pop a piece of dry pasta in your mouth and when the moment is right, stand up, shake your head from side to side, then with one hand pretend to push your head to the side. At the same time crunch the pasta. It will sound as if you have cracked your neck like a fully fledged weight-lifter!

Can and string telephone   This is not an illusion, it really works. If you never made one of these when you were a kid, then shame on you. Where is your scientific endeavour?

Simply get two tin cans and make a hole in the bottom of each. Then thread a long string through each and knot it so that it cannot come out. Then you and whoever you want to talk to on the telephone stretch the string to its limit (experiment to see how far you can go) and with it fairly taught speak into your can while the other person listens.

Amplify your sound with two umbrellas   Simply open up two umbrellas and position them about five or six metres apart so that they are pointing at each other. You can try having a conversation with a friend by umbrella, or you can see if you can amplify the sound of a clock or a bell by putting it in the middle of one.

THE FIRST PHONE CALL

In 1876 Alexander Graham Bell and his assistant transmitted the first telephone message. Bell was in one room and called his assistant in another room with the words 'Watson, come here; I want you.' In the following year he set up the Bell Telephone Company, which developed a local telephone exchange. In 1973 the first mobile phone call was made.

TOUCH

The sense of touch is very complicated, depending on a whole range of different nerve end receptors and different pathways to the brain. I am going to try and keep this as simple as possible.

Look at the diagram of the brain. This shows the left side of the brain in profile, so that the person would be looking to the left. The shaded area

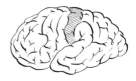

The post-central gyrus and the sensory homunculus

is called the post-central gyrus and is predominantly to do with the perception of touch and temperature. Over the years we have mapped out how much of that area is devoted to the different parts of the body. As a result we can effectively produce a map that is called the **sensory homunculus.** That is, the relative areas of the brain that are devoted to sensation give an impression of how the brain 'sees' the body. It is effectively like a small person with big feet, huge hands, a large head with prominent eyes, ears and nose and a big tongue. This can be seen on the cross section diagram next to the left side view. And if you think about it, that is what it feels like, although our brains give us a more aesthetic perception of ourselves.

In medicine we test a person's **two-point discrimination,** or ability to detect the gap between two points by touching his or her skin with two sharp pins at the same time. It is rather like a using a pair of geometry dividers to measure a distance between. The fingers and thumbs have masses of nerve receptors so you can discriminate between two very, very close points, while the trunk and shoulders are not very sensitive at all, and you may not detect a difference between two points inches apart.

Fool your sense of touch

There is an old party trick called the clothes-brush stunt that you may like to try out. You approach someone with a clothes-brush and offer to brush his or her clothes. It is best if you have an audience because it is quite effective. Tell the person to hold his or her head up and look straight ahead. You go behind and start to brush your own cloths, at the same time gently stroking the person's shoulders and back with your hand. Thus, your clothes get brushed, but the person will not realize it. The reason is that the two-point discrimination and sense of touch in general over that area is pretty poor. You then tell the person and he or she may be quite surprised, but should find it quite funny as well.

And this is another interesting one that you can do on yourself. I call it

The two noses illusion

Hot or cold?

the two noses illusion. If you cross your fingers and rub your nose with your eyes closed, you will feel two noses!

Hot or cold?

Our ability to detect hot and cold is generally very sensitive, but it too can be fooled.

Get three bowls and fill one with water that is as hot as you can comfortably manage; one with water that is as cold as you can comfortably manage; and one with water that is in between the two. It is easiest to measure out two equal quantities of the other two and put them together in another bowl.

Dip one hand in the hot and one in the cold and keep them there for one minute. Now put one in the warm and see what you feel. Then put the other in the warm and compare it. You will find that the one that was in the hot initially will feel that the middle bowl is cold, while the one that was in the cold will feel that the middle bowl is hot.

BALANCE

Your sense of balance is more complex than you may imagine. Although I mentioned that the semi-circular canals in the ear help us to balance, they do not do it alone. The brain keeps you balanced by combining information from three sources.

Firstly, from the semi-circular canals. There are three of them set at right angles to one another, so that movement in any one of three planes will send signals to the brain, so that you can correct where your body is, if you desire.

Secondly, from your vision. Your visual signals help to build a bigger picture. It is easier to balance with your eyes open.

Lastly, from special little receptors in your joints and muscles. These are called proprioceptors and they send signals to the brain about where your limbs are in space at any time.

You probably utilize the information from these sources to help you balance in the respective proportions of 60, 30 and 10 per cent.

So why can't we all be tight-rope artists?

Well, possibly you could. When you think about it you can probably walk along a straight line. I expect you have walked along the kerbstones of a pavement without any problem whatsoever. With a wall a couple of feet off the ground you are probably also OK. But when you get to your own height your mind starts to kick in and flashes danger signals. You may be reluctant to try this, which is good. So could you walk on a tight-rope over the Niagara Falls?

It is the brain that creates the difficulty – or sees the danger! Let's not try and fool this sense.

CHAPTER EIGHTEEN

MÖBIUS BANDS
... AND THE AMAZING WORLD OF
TOPOLOGY

When I was a youngster I used to hang out in a saddlery shop. It was not that I was remotely interested in leatherwork or saddle-making, it was simply that for no very good reason at all they also sold magic tricks. One of the very first that I bought was called the Afghan bands. I remember buying it because it sounded incredibly exotic. And when I took it home and tried it out, to my nine-year-old brain it actually seemed to be magic.

The Afghan
bands

Let me describe the effect to you, pretty much as it was described on the magic trick packet.

> The conjurer has three ribbon bands or loops hanging on his wrist and in his other hand he holds three pairs of scissors. He invites two people on stage to help him. He tells them that he wants them to duplicate what he does, and that if they can do it exactly the same way, he will give them a reward. He hands each of them a ribbon loop and a pair of scissors. He then cuts his band along its length and – not surprisingly – ends up with two bands.
>
> To the amazement of the audience his helpers are unable to duplicate this simple cutting. The first ends up with a single ribbon band twice as long as the original. And even more surprisingly, the other helper ends up with two ribbon bands which are mysteriously linked together.

Now, I practised this and obtained exactly the result that was promised. There is a secret, of course, and that is in the preparation of the ribbon loops. Three loops are made. The first one simply has both ends glued together to form an ordinary loop. The second has one half-twist before gluing the ends. The third has two half-twists before gluing the ends. When these are cut along their lengths, you will find that they respectively produce one large ring and two rings linked together.

It amazed me then and it still amazes me. Try it out yourself and see if you can fathom it out.

THE MÖBIUS BAND

If you didn't work it out straight away, don't worry. It has been a curio of the branch of mathematics known as topology for a long time. The principle behind this magic trick – and I subsequently found out that it was the legendary illusionist Professor Louis Hoffman who named it the Afghan Bands Illusion when he performed it in about 1904 – was actually first described by August Ferdinand Möbius (1790–1868), a German mathematician and astronomer, in 1858.

The Möbius band (or strip) that is named after him, and which is created by giving a half-twist to one end of a band before sealing the ends, actually *has only one surface*!

To be slightly technical, a *Möbius band* is a non-orientable two-dimensional surface with only one side when embedded in three-dimensional Euclidean space.

The loop with one half-twist (twisted through 180°) is a Möbius band. The others are not.

Möbius band properties

You really ought to make a Möbius band and examine it as you go. Firstly, get a pen and try drawing a line down its middle from the seam. Keep going without taking the pen off the paper and you will find that you eventually meet the original starting point. That might seem incredible.

Now if you go to the edge of the band and follow that edge all the way along between your fingers (you will have a little manipulation to do this through the loop) you will find that it only has one edge. That will possibly seem even more incredible.

Now get a pair of scissors and cut down the middle of the band, starting at the seam. Keep cutting until you reach the original point. You will find that you now have a band that is twice as long, but thinner. It is not a Möbius band because it has two half twists. Try drawing a line around this one and you will find that it actually has two surfaces, not one. And if you feel along the edge, you will find that it has two edges, not one. The reason is that you just cut an extra edge.

OK, so now try cutting along the middle of this new large loop. You will find that you now get two loops joined together.

And that, you may have guessed, is the essence of the magic trick called the Afghan bands. You started with three loops. One was a normal one that cut into two separate loops. The second was a Möbius band that cut into a larger loop. The third was a smaller version of the big loop that resulted from a cut Möbius band.

There is another interesting phenomenon that you can check out. If you cut a Möbius band a third of the way from the edge, rather than halfway, you will get one Möbius band of the same size as the original, only thinner. But it will be interlinked with a larger band twice as big, which will be like the big loop that you would have made had you cut down the middle. It will have two half twists and will not be a Möbius band.

The fourth dimension

If you take two mirror-image Möbius bands (bands with the twists in the opposite direction,[25] one a clockwise half twist and the other an anti-clockwise half twist), then no matter how you try to deform them, you cannot superimpose one on top of the other. Not in Euclidean space, that is. That means not in the space that we live in and orientate everything within. But if you could take the bands into four-dimensional space, then you could make the transformation.

This is because the two bands are considered to be topologically equivalent, even if they are mirror images here. Topological equivalence is a concept that two objects may seem completely different, yet by continuous deformation they can be transformed into each other. A mug and a doughnut, for example, could be transformed into one another, whereas a ball and a doughnut could not. The first two are topologically equivalent, but the latter two are not.

> A band with an odd number of half twists, like the Möbius band, will have only one edge and one surface. A band with an even number of half twists will have two edges and two surfaces.

A better Afghan band illusion

OK, now that you have the idea of the Möbius band, here's a different way of performing this trick. It has an advantage in that you can do this on your own without helpers. It works best with a cloth ribbon rather than paper, for reasons that will be obvious.

Get a good-sized ribbon and make a slit of one inch in the middle of one end. Make a similar slit in the other end, but make it three inches long. Bring the ends towards one another as if to make a loop. But with one of the halves from the long slit end make a half twist through 180° and glue this to its waiting half on the other end. Then with the other half from the long slit end make two half twists (twisting through 360°) and glue it to the waiting half on the other end. Let it all dry and then you are ready to perform.

You tell your audience that you have a loop of ribbon, which you are going to tear down the middle. You tell them that this will, of course, result in two bands. But, master magician that you are, you can make mysterious things happen. Taking the loop with the double half twist you tear this down the middle to produce two interlinked rings.

Your audience will be amazed and puzzled at these. So you then direct their attention to the remaining loop – the Möbius band – and tear this, telling them that magic makes the unexpected happen. And this time, instead of the interlinked rings, you show them the large loop.

You take a bow, enjoy their adulation – then, if you feel like it, you can explain the science to them.

Infinity

I am sure that you know the symbol for infinity – ∞. The origin of the symbol is unclear, but one of the theories is that it relates to a Möbius band, which you could walk down the middle of and never come to an end. I would love to end this chapter as if that were so, because I think it is an apposite symbol. But sadly, I cannot. The symbol was in use a couple of hundred years before August Ferdinand Möbius came along to enlighten (and bamboozle) us.

The infinity symbol is actually credited to John Wallis (1616–1703), a distinguished English mathematician. He used the symbol in his book *De sectionibus conicis*, published in 1655.

An unknown wit ...

... left us this limerick.

A mathematician confided
That a Möbius strip is one-sided.
You'll get quite a laugh
If you cut it in half,
For it stays in one piece when divided.

CHAPTER NINETEEN

WEIRD STUFF!

You might think that this is an odd chapter heading. Well, it is, but don't let that put you off. I am going to consider a few areas that defy scientific explanation, but which are certainly worthy of scientific investigation. Indeed, you can subject them to your own experimentation and decide whether you think there is anything in them or not.

And that is a good exercise in science.

THE GREAT PYRAMID MYSTERY

Think of Egypt and you almost inevitably think about the pyramids. They are dotted all over the country and they inspire awe in everyone who sees them. Many of them were built as tombs for the pharaohs and their consorts, the others being built for some of the nobility. It is believed that there was a gradual evolution in design from the early flat-topped

Making a
pyramid

mastabas, or bench-like tomb structures, of the ancient days. The first recognizable pyramid is the step-pyramid of King Djoser at Saqqara, the first king of the third dynasty. It was built in about 2,600BC by his grand vizier Imhotep, a priest, physician and architect who was later deified as a god of medicine. This pyramid consists of six mastabas built one on top of the other to produce the famous step-pyramid structure.

To date there are 138 pyramids in Egypt, but none elicit as much wonder as the 3 pyramids of the Giza plateau, outside Cairo. Along with the Sphinx, the pyramids of Khufu, Khafre and Menkaure epitomize the mystery of Egypt. That of Khufu, the Great Pyramid, is the last of the Seven Wonders of the World still in existence. It is perhaps for this reason that it evokes such wonder.

The Great Pyramid

The Great Pyramid stands on the Giza plateau. It was the tallest man-made structure on earth for almost four millennia. Incredibly, the four sides of the base have a mean error of only 58 millimeters in length. The base is horizontal and flat to within 21 millimetres and the sides of the square base are closely aligned to the four cardinal compass points based on true north.

Over the centuries there have been many theories about the Great Pyramid. Some of them have been highly speculative, and some seem utterly zany. There are theories about how it was built and what its function was. Some 'pyramidologists' even claim that encoded within its structure there are predictions about the whole future history of humans on earth.

I have no intention of saying more than that. If it interests you then there is lots of information that you can root out. Here, we want to consider a potentially interesting phenomenon that you can investigate yourself. It is said to relate to the curious internal geometry of the Great Pyramid.

In the 1930s a Frenchman by the name of Antoine Bovis reported that a cat had been found that had wandered into the King's Chamber of the Great Pyramid and died. Its body became mummified. This stimulated Bovis to investigate the geometry of the pyramid and to experiment with models built to the exact dimensions of the Great Pyramid.

In 1949 a Czechoslovakian engineer called Karel Drbal applied for a patent for a cardboard model of the Great Pyramid, which he said could sharpen used razor blades. 'Pyramid Power' then achieved a remarkable popularity, which peaked in the 1970 and 1980s as interest in New Age literature and pursuits swept the world. Several eminent scientists looked at this curious idea and many people constructed their own cardboard pyramids to test it themselves. And seemingly, many people obtained surprising results.

It is said that a cardboard model of the Great Pyramid can in some way harness a mysterious energy that can 'preserve' flowers and fruits, sharpen knives, scissors and old-fashioned razor blades.

I actually tried this with a cardboard pyramid and set up a 'control' with a box. I put white seedless grapes under the pyramid and the same number under the box. After a week I had raisins under the pyramid, but just rotting grapes under the box. That wasn't a terribly scientific experiment, but it was enough to get me setting up more experiments.

But I will say no more about my results, because this is an opportunity for you to try out your own experiments to see if you can uncover the mystery of the pyramid – or not, as the case may be.

Pyramid Experiments

Firstly, make your pyramid. I would suggest making one with a base of six inches, which will give you a large enough model to test. Get four pieces of cardboard. Make a triangle on each, with a base of 6 inches and sides of 5.7 inches. Tape them together and you will have a pyramid of about 4 inches in height. This will be the same geometrical shape as the Great Pyramid of Giza. Next get a larger piece of hardboard or cardboard to use as a base. One of about 10 to 12 inches will be quite adequate. Align the pyramid so that the four faces point exactly in the direction of the four cardinal points.

Now you are ready to begin. You can either place objects that you want to test on the base and cover with the pyramid, or (and some people claim that this is better) get a small box that comes up to a little more that inch and a half in height: that is, about a third of the height of the pyramid. Use this as a plinth to place your specimens.

For a control, get a box with base sides of about 6 inches each and around 4 inches in height, with or without a plinth (depending on whether you have one in the pyramid).

Then try your own experiments with flowers, various fruits (I recommend grapes) and perhaps a couple of equally blunt knives.

These are not short experiments, by the way. You may be setting them up for a couple of weeks or a month at a time. But be scientific, make regular observations, perhaps weigh your specimens, and record everything.

And come to your own conclusions.

EXTRA-SENSORY PERCEPTION AND PSYCHOKINESIS

There have been reports of paranormal phenomena in virtually every culture since the beginnings of recorded history. Of course, in the scientific age there is a tendency to write such phenomena off as superstition, coincidence or fraud, yet the very fact that people are aware of them and that they are considered outwith normal and everyday events means that there is a legitimate reason to study them.

The first systematic study of these phenomena began in 1882, when the Society for Psychical Research was founded in London by the philosopher Henry Sedgwick. His co-founders were the physicists Sir Oliver Lodge, Sir William Barrett and Sir William Crookes, and the philosophers Frederick WH Myers and Edmund Gurney. In 1885, following a meeting between Sedgwick and the psychologist William James, a twin organization came into being with the founding of the American Society for Psychical Research. The early focus of research for both societies was in the growing field of spiritualism and mediumship.

The first effective scientific research into psychic phenomena began in the 1920s, under the direction of Professor Joseph B Rhine (1895–1980) in the psychology department at Duke University, North Carolina. This was to be the beginning of a new branch of psychology.

Rhine took a quite different approach from the early psychic researchers by studying 'everyday' people rather than professed psychics. His hypothesis was that if psychic abilities exist, then they should be apparent within the general population. Accordingly, his first subjects were recruited from the student body at Duke.

Initially, Rhine wanted to study telepathic ability using playing cards. It became clear to him, however, that 52 separate 'symbols' were possibly too many to deal with, but that some subjects might subconsciously over-select favourite cards or reject particular numbers they were superstitious about. A colleague, Karl Zenner, came up with the solution by producing a deck of 25 cards, consisting of 5 cards each of 5 different symbols. These were a square, a circle, a star, a set of wavy lines and a plus sign.

In the classic Rhine experiments the subject tries to perceive the order of the five symbols when they are randomly shuffled. Since the chance of predicting a symbol is one in five, it is a relatively easy matter to calculate the probability of achieving particular scores. Sometimes the experiments were conducted facing the subject over a table, sometimes in a different room and sometimes in different buildings.

Rhine found some subjects were particularly adept with the Zenner cards, consistently producing results that were statistically significant. In 1934 he published his research in a monograph entitled *Extra-Sensory Perception*. His choice of the term had been carefully made, since he

The Zenner cards

postulated that the perception was outwith the usual five senses. Now here is your opportunity to see if you or your family has ESP.

The Zenner cards   You can buy a deck of Zenner cards at any magical dealer. Alternatively, they are very simple to make. Just get 25 plain file cards and draw 5 of each of these symbols on them: waves, square, circle, star, cross.

The Telepathy Experiment

You will need two of you, one to act as a sender and the other to be the receiver. Has the receiver got ESP?

REQUIREMENTS

- ✓ a Zenner deck of cards
- ✓ a quiet room with no distractions
- ✓ pad and pencil to record results

METHOD

You should first of all decide how many trials you are going to do, each trial being a run-through of the entire deck of 25 cards. I would suggest four trials to make the calculation easy (and the more you do the more significant will your results be), but I will run through this with you in the results section.

The two people can be in the same room, they can be facing each other across a table, or they can even be in different rooms. The receiver should not be able to see the cards.

The sender should shuffle the cards well and place the deck on the table. Then he or she should look at the top card, concentrate on it and try to 'send' the image to the receiver, then place the card face down beside the deck, to form a used pile. The receiver tries to 'see' the symbol in the sender's mind. He or she then says what he or she thinks the symbol is. The sender records what the symbol was and whether the receiver scored a hit (✓) or a miss (✗). This should be done behind a screen, or with the pad on the knee below the table, so that the receiver can get no clue about the result. Go though the whole deck and however many trials you want to. The cards should be thoroughly shuffled at the end of each trial. If the receiver is tired, then stop and restart when he or she is ready to continue.

Then count up the correct score and do the calculation to see whether the receiver seems to have ESP or not.

You can go on from there and swap roles to test the sender's ESP ability. The thing is to treat it as a serious experiment.

RESULTS

Dr Rhine used a mathematical formula to calculate the 'critical ratio', which will give you a fairly good indication of whether the receiver is scoring better than chance.

So here we go:

The odds of being correct for any card are 1 in 5, or 1/5	= 0.2
The total number of predictions	= p
Add up the number of hits	= h
Calculate the average score, or the score that would be achieved by chance. This is obtained by multiplying p by 0.2 p x 0.2	=a

Now work out these two figures (quite obvious really):

Firstly, 1 minus the odds of being correct, or 1-0.2	= 0.8
Secondly, the product of 0.8 and your odds of being correct, or 0.8 x 0.2	= 0.16 = b

Calculate the product of the total number of predictions p and **b**	= pb
Use a calculator to get the square root of **pb**	= $\sqrt{pb}$
Subtract the average score **a** from the number of hits **h**	= h-a
Divide this by the square root of **pb** to get the critical ratio **m**	

Thus   **m**   = h-a / $\sqrt{pb}$

I hope that doesn't seem too complicated. But if we run through it, saying that you did 4 trials of 25 cards and therefore 100 predictions, it should seem quite straightforward.

The odds of being correct for any card are 1 in 5, or 1/5	= 0.2
The total number of predictions	p = 100

Suppose the number of hits was 36 (a very good score) $\qquad$ **h = 36**

Calculate the average score, or the score that would be achieved by chance

p x 0.2 = a		= 20
Calculate **b**, as above		= 0.16
Therefore	pb	= 16
Therefore if	m	= h-a / $\sqrt{pb}$
Then	m	= 36-20/ $\sqrt{16}$
Thus	m	= 16/4
	m	= 4

Now comes the interesting bit, which reveals all. If **m** is

less than 1.96 =		no psychic ability
1.96 to 2.58 =		perhaps psychic ability
2.58 to 3.00 =		significant psychic ability
over 3.00 =		very significant psychic ability

The Precognition Experiment

Here, very simply, you can test yourself. Simply shuffle the deck and place it in front of you on the table. Pick up one card at a time and record what you think it is, then place it on the bottom of the deck. Go through the whole 25, making sure that you do not see any of the cards, and making sure that you place each card on the bottom, so that you will retain the order of the deck. Then turn over one by one to see how many hits you achieved.

As before, decide ahead of the experiment how many trials you are going to do, remembering that the more you do the more significant the result. Calculate your critical ratio as before. Then make your own conclusion.

DOWSING

I want to introduce you to another interesting subject, which you can experiment freely with and make up your own mind as to whether there is something there or not. This is dowsing, or the practice of finding things by relying upon the movement of some inanimate object, which is held in the hands of the operator.

Dowsing is a collective term for a number of practices ranging from simple water-divining or water-detecting, the detection of pipes, electrical cables, archaeological remains or even the location of missing persons.

Radiesthesia is the name for the study of the dowsing phenomenon. Whereas dowsing basically accepts and does not imply a questioning of the nature of the phenomenon, radiesthesia attempts to explain and advance the subject as a scientific discipline. The word radiesthesia was first coined by the French Abbé Bouley from the Latin *radiare*, meaning ray or emission of rays; and the Greek *aisthanesthai*, meaning to perceive. As such the original implication was that in some way the individual perceives something that emanates like a radiation from the object under study.

Dowsing is a practice that stretches back at least to the days of the Ancient Egyptians. Tomb paintings clearly illustrate priests using forked sticks to dowse. Similarly, artefacts from Ancient China prove that the divining rod was known and used in the Imperial courts. Going even further back, neolithic cave paintings discovered in north-west Africa are suggestive of the use of dowsing as long ago as 7,000 to 8,000 years ago.

The mystical rod

Dowsing was known to most ancient cultures. In antiquity, dowsers mostly used some form of rod or wand. Indeed, the traditional name for dowsing and water-divining was **rhabdomancy**, from the Greek *rhabdos*, meaning rod.

The fact that dowsing was probably regarded as the domain of the shaman or sorcerer–priest survives in the main attribute of the popular image of the witch, wizard and magician – the magic wand.

'The rod' has been the standard tool for dowsing water, minerals and ores over the centuries. Indeed, its use is mentioned in various texts written by monks during the Dark Ages. In 1556, Georgius Agricola, a physician and the founding father of the science of mineralogy, wrote a book entitled *De Re Metallica*. In it he discusses the use of the divining rod in searching for mineral veins. An illustration in the book even shows a dowser working with a forked hazel branch.

Perhaps as a result of that work the use of dowsers spread across Europe. The growth of the tin mining industry in Cornwall, England, is even thought to owe much to the dowser's art. During the Elizabethan age German miners were brought over and commissioned to dowse for tin veins.

Over the next century, however, dowsing by and large fell into disrepute. The church considered it to be the work of the devil. Indeed, it is fair to say that the practice of dowsing could put an individual in peril of the Inquisition.

The dowsing L rods

Make your own L rods

This is easily done by getting two metal coat-hangers and unwinding the hooks, then clipping the curly bits off. If you then snip one at the end of the long section and bend the other end so that you have a 90° angle, then you have an L rod. Repeat the process with the other hanger and you have a pair. Next take two straws and slip these over the shorter arms so that they move freely. You now simply hold them in front of you and you are ready to experiment.

How to test them

You are supposed to ask a question in your mind and form a mental image. Thus, if your question is about finding water, you formulate the question 'Is there water here?' and picture water. You then move forward and the L rods should provide you with information – if you have a dowsing ability! And that is what you are aiming to find out, is it not?

The L rods will either do nothing, or begin to move within their straws. If the answer is 'yes' they will cross over. If they are directing you towards water, as you move forward they will both possibly point in the same direction, eventually crossing over or flying in opposite directions (and the response you may get may be personal) when you arrive at water.

And so, you can test this out by trying to trace water pipes, or you could try to trace underground stonework, or the positions of underground or underfloor cables. You formulate the questions and you make your own conclusions. You may find that nothing happens or you may find that something happens, and that could be enough to make you want to explore this some more.

The pendulum

The Romans developed the art of **dactylomancy**, or pendulum dowsing. At the College of Augurs in Rome[26] they taught the use of swinging finger rings on fine threads in order to divine answers. Hence the term meant finger divination, from the word *dactulos*, meaning finger.

Although the rod has been the universal field-method for dowsing, the pendulum is used by many dowsers for indoor work.

Much of the early work in the twentieth century was done in France. As mentioned earlier, the Abbé Bouley introduced the term radiesthesia. Both he and another cleric, the Abbé Mermet, trained many radiesthetists in the practice in the years after the Great War.

Mermet in particular became greatly renowned and attracted clients from every corner of the world. His book, *Principles and Practice of Radiesthesia*, was to become the standard work on the subject.

Tintin and Professor Calculus

I first came across *The Adventures of Tintin* when I was at school and I have been a fan of the stories ever since. These wonderful stories were created, written and illustrated by the Belgian artist Georges Rémi (1907–1983), who wrote under the pen-name of Hergé.

Tintin is a young reporter who has many adventures in many lands, and indeed even in space and on the moon. In these he is aided by his dog Snowy and his great friends Captain Haddock and Professor Calculus. The professor is a wonderful character whose hardness of hearing creates many

Tintin's friend Professor Calculus is an enthusiastic dowser © **Hergé/Moulinsart** 2010

hilarious situations. But make no mistake – he is a scientific genius who invents several splendid inventions that are of great help in their adventures. In addition to this, he is an enthusiastic pendulum dowser, which is apparent in several of the tales.

I felt that if it was good enough for Professor Cuthbert Calculus then there had to be something in this mysterious pendulum. In short, it was a subject worthy of study.

Make A Pendulum

The pendulum itself, as the name suggests, consists of a weight or bob suspended by thread or fine chain. A length of about 10 centimetres is convenient while a bob may be of any material such as crystal, glass, plastic or wood. I would suggest hanging a nut (as in nut and bolt) from a thread or a thin cord, such as fishing line.

PENDULUM MOVEMENTS

There are three basic movements, namely:

1. A simple to-and-fro oscillation, usually, but not necessarily, towards and away from the operator.
2. A rotary motion in a clockwise direction.
3. A similar rotary movement anticlockwise.

Make a pendulum
from a weight on
a string

It is these movements or combinations thereof that are said to provide the answers to the questions being posed. For example, 'yes' might be a clockwise circle, 'no' might be an anti-clockwise circle, and an oscillation could be a 'maybe'.

Dowsers say that you can determine the sex of an individual, or that of a newborn chick or even of an egg by the pendulum responses. You have to establish your own sex indicator responses first.

This little experiment might convince you whether there is anything in it. Get a number of paper slips and write boys' names and girls' names on them. Put them in envelopes and mix them up. Ask the pendulum, 'Does this name belong to a boy or a girl?'

I say no more. Make up your own mind.

Mind-Reading Made Simple

OK, so we shall take a break from dowsing experiments and delve a little deeper into the mysteries of the mind. Mind-reading, I mean. I am sure that you will have seen professional magicians reading people's minds with apparent ease in situations so controlled that it is impossible to come to any other conclusion than that they can read minds. Or do they?

The mysterious coin

Of course not! They are providing entertainment. Telepathy may exist – you may already have demonstrated that you or a friend or relative has it, at least to your own satisfaction – but it does not seem to be something that can be done on demand.

Well, would you like a quick lesson in mind-reading?

You would? Well then, all you need is an old coin, something like a florin or a half crown. Both are good because they are quite heavy and good to hold in the hand. I suggest an old one, because that looks just a little bit mysterious. As an alternative, you could use an old penny or even an old Chinese coin. One of those with a square hole in the middle.

You will need a little practice to get your patter right. But once armed, you are in a position to do three very neat routines.

A WORD OF ADVICE

Do not repeat a trick, no matter how many times people beg you to. Do it once then leave it. It is much more effective and mysterious that way. It will also make it less likely that someone will work out how you did it!

Instant Mind-Reading
This little trick is a stunner, and works virtually automatically in 95 per cent of cases.

EFFECT
You first of all talk about ESP and explain that you have been conducting your own research. So far your research has been quite revealing and you have developed an ability to locate a coin wherever it is.

You then show your coin and hand it to someone and tell him or her to put it behind his or her back and place it in one hand, then close each hand into a fist and bring both hands to the front. Ask the person to then hold his or her hands out in front and slowly separate them, concentrating all the time on the coin.

You are immediately able to predict the hand that the coin is hidden in.

EXPLANATION
Very simply, the person will give him or herself away unconsciously. Do not look at the hands, but the face. As the person separates his or her hands the nose will point to the hand containing the coin. Some people will also make a small eye movement in that direction.

Try it and be amazed.

Coin Precognition
Wouldn't it be good to be able to predict whether a coin falls heads or tails? you ask your audience. Then you tell them that because of your studies into ESP you have been able to do just that.

EFFECT
Showing your coin, you spin it on the table like a top. Then you immediately pick it up. You tell the audience that you are in tune with the ether and that you can tell whether the coin will fall heads or tails. You direct one person to take the coin and spin it while you turn your back. You say that you will then tell him how it has landed.

You will be correct, of course.

EXPLANATION
This is where you have to doctor the coin beforehand and do a little practice. You simply cut a small notch on the edge of one side. It needs to be allowed to darken again, so that it does not look contrived. No one will notice it. I suspect you barely noticed it in the photograph, did you? It is at the six o'clock position.

The coin will sound different as it settles down after a spin. The notched side will sound flat and have a clicky quality. The other side will have a ringing sound. This is where the practice comes in. Keep spinning it until you recognize the difference automatically. Hence you will be able to make the prediction every time.

Dowsing The Coin

This final trick links with the dowsing pendulum and can be used as the third trick in your repertoire of mind-reading experiments. In fact this one is a combination of dowsing and mind-reading. As with the last trick, you will need to do a little practice, but this time with the pendulum.

REQUIREMENTS

✓ a pendulum, as described earlier
✓ your mysterious coin

EFFECT

This stunt requires a number of people and a table. Four or more people are ideal for this trick, but the more the better. You explain about your research into dowsing with the pendulum. Tell them how it is used to sex chickens and so forth. And then tell them that a little demonstration with your mysterious coin may help to explain this amazing phenomenon.

You lay your mysterious coin on the table and tell them that you are going to leave the room for half a minute. While you have gone one of the group should hold the coin in one fist and place this fist against his or her

Coin divination

forehead for 20 seconds and concentrate on the coin, sending a message into the ether that he or she has the coin in one hand.

After the 20 seconds they all lay their hands on the table, with closed fists, and call you back into the room. Your pendulum whirls and leads you unerringly to the hand holding the coin.

EXPLANATION

You can, if you want, and if you have felt that you have dowsing talent, let the pendulum guide you.

Alternatively, you can just let the pendulum seem to lead you. And that is where the practice comes in. You have to make the pendulum seem to drag your hand to the coin.

The hand holding the coin will have revealed itself, since it would be the one that was markedly white when you entered the room. Certainly it will have been the whiter of someone's pair of hands. But note that quickly, before you begin your routine with the pendulum, since it will colour back to normal soon enough.

The flushing toilet question

I wondered about the wisdom of exploring this topic, but toilets are part of everyday life and the question we are going to consider is bound to come up in conversation sometime or another. It is this – does the toilet flush in one direction in the northern hemisphere and in the opposite in the southern?

In fairness, you can draw the question out and include the direction in which a sink drains in the two hemispheres.

Strangely enough this is one of those questions that you would think was easy to find the answer to, yet it still provokes discussion and argument, even amongst scientists.

Apparently if you go on a cruise across the equator (which I admit that I have never done) you will almost certainly be shown the phenomenon whereby a bucket with a hole in it is allowed to drain. While you are north of the equator the bucket will empty in a clockwise direction and as you reach the equator it will swirl one way or the other, but as you go south the swirling will be anti-clockwise.

If this hasn't already had you running to check the toilet flush or the way that your sink drains, please do so now.

A SHORT HISTORY OF THE FLUSHING TOILET

- The Indian cities of Harappa and Mohendaro had flushing toilets in 2,600BC

- The Romans used flushing toilets throughout their empire, from the first to the fifth century AD. You can see one at Vindolanda, a Roman garrison town close to Hadrian's Wall
- In 1596 Sir John Harrington installed a flush toilet at Richmond Palace for Queen Elizabeth I. Apparently she didn't like to use it because of the noise!
- In 1775 Alexander Cummings invented the S bend, which allowed standing water to act as a seal to prevent the backward escape of unpleasant odours
- In 1819 Albert Giblin patented a siphon discharge system
- The first public flushing toilets were installed at the Crystal Palace. The charge to use them was one penny, hence the expression 'to spend a penny'
- In the 1880s Thomas Crapper & Co, a plumbing company started building flush toilets, using Giblin's design
- In 1906 Thomas MacAvity Stewart invented the vortex flushing toilet bowl

The Coriolis effect

This curious phenomenon is said to come about because of the Coriolis force, which was first described in 1835 by Gaspard-Gustave de Coriolis (1792–1843), a French mathematician and engineer. It is all to do with rotating reference frames. It is quite complex, but in a nutshell, because the earth is a sphere rotating about its axis, a point on the equator is moving much faster than points to the north and the south. At the equator the earth is moving at a speed of about 1,670 kilometres per hour, but at the poles it is a gentle, very slow spin. The air above is travelling at the same speed, but if it is moving northwards it will slow down and curve to the right. If it is travelling south it will curve to the left.

This seems to account for storms, which turn clockwise in the northern hemisphere and anti-clockwise south of the equator.

And this same force. The Coriolis force is said to affect draining water. It will swirl clockwise in the northern hemisphere and anti-clockwise in the southern.

The flushing toilet experiment

But does it?

Well, this is for you to put to the test, whenever you watch a toilet flush, or a bath or sink drain. And do it scientifically. Record your observations over a period of time. The thing is that many people are not convinced that the Coriolis force would have an effect on something as small as a bath, a toilet or a sink. It could be to do with the direction of water entering, the design of the emptying container or even the speed of the flow.

What do you think?

MURPHY'S LAW

This is another curious one. I am sure that you will have heard of Murphy's Law, which states that 'If anything can go wrong, it will go wrong.'

It sounds like the ultimate pessimist's maxim, doesn't it? Yet strangely, scientists have devoted a lot of time to it. Indeed, in 2001 a nationwide experiment was done to study this by the simple means of looking at whether or not a slice of buttered toast would tend to fall from a plate and land on its buttered side. Children in schools across the country conducted 10,000 trials and found that toast landed butter-side down 62 per cent of the time. That is a significant result, since it should only occur 50 per cent of the time according to chance.

Interestingly, the presence of butter actually does not seem to affect the results. It does not appreciably alter the weight or the aerodynamics.

Height seems to be the issue, since the toast does not have enough falling room to turn over 360°. It has been worked out that it would need to fall from about eight feet to have a decent chance of landing butter-side up.

So there you go: an experiment that you can easily replicate. You need to have an adequate number of trials, of course. The rest I leave up to you. (Oh, it is not a bad idea to put newspapers down on the floor before you begin!)

Murphy's Law!

CHAPTER TWENTY

THE THEORY OF EVERYTHING
... WHICH COMES AT THE END

Up until the 1990s it was almost universally agreed by theoretical physicists that all matter was made up of atoms and sub-atomic particles, which were held together by four fundamental forces.

First was the **gravitational force,** which keeps our feet on the earth, stops the sun from exploding and the galaxies from scattering. Second was the **electromagnetic force,** which we harness to power our lights, our homes and our cities. Third was the **weak nuclear force,** which is responsible for radioactive decay. This we use in nuclear medicine, in the use of radioactive tracers in our highly sophisticated diagnostic scanners. Fourth was the **strong nuclear force,** which is demonstrated by the power of the sun, the power within the atom. In 1979 Sheldon Lee Glashow, Steven Weinberg and Abdus Salam were awarded the Nobel Prize for Physics for their work in showing that the weak nuclear force and the electromagnetic force were manifestations of a single force, called the **electroweak force.**

The way in which these three fundamental forces operate is of monumental importance in science. But just what is their connection? Indeed, can they all be unified into a single super-force?

There are two main theories, which have each partially explained the nature of these forces. One is the **quantum theory,** as outlined by Niels Henrik David Bohr (1885–1962), and the other is **general relativity,** as formulated by Albert Einstein (1879–1955). They deal with opposite ends of the spectrum, however, because quantum

String theory may hold the answer!

theory deals with the realm of the microcosm, the subatomic world, whereas general relativity explains the macrocosm, the nature of the Big Bang, galaxies and black holes. Quantum theory explains forces as packets or quanta of energy, whereas general relativity explains forces as deformations of space–time. Interestingly, you can take either one and derive all of the laws of physics and chemistry from it. You can build the entire scientific edifice from one of the theories – but not from both!

This vexing problem consumed all of Albert Einstein's energy over the last 30 years of his life. He pursued a theory that he never finished, but which he proposed to call the **unified field theory**. Effectively, it was to be a theory of the universe. It is a quest that has absorbed the careers of countless theoretical physicists since then.

In the 1970s and 1980s it looked as if a possible solution had presented itself with the development of **superstring theory**. The basis of this theory was that all matter is composed of superstrings, which occupy a single point in space–time at any one time. This seemed compatible with both quantum theory and general relativity, except that it could only work if there were 10 dimensions. However, the **Kaluza–Klein theory** allows for this possibility if the extra dimensions (other than the three spatial ones and the one of time) are curled up into an infinitely small space. It was conjectured that just before the Big Bang, there was an empty, but unstable, 10-dimensional universe. This split into two fragments, our known four-dimensional universe and a six-dimensional universe. The universe made the quantum leap to another universe causing the six dimensions to curl up and the four-dimensional universe to expand. This rapid expansion at some point caused the Big Bang. Current thinking is that rather than this being the creation of everything, it was in fact an aftershock of the collapse of the 10-dimensional universe.

There have been five 'string' theories to date, culminating in the unification of them into a single **M-theory** in 1994. However, M-theory only holds true if there were 11 dimensions. Indeed, theoretical physicists are now talking about the possibility of a twelfth dimension.

With these mind-boggling theories (which are of course not testable, because it is impossible to measure dimensions that are smaller than an atom) it would have seemed that a **grand unification theory** or **Theory of Everything** had been achieved. Or at least a Theory of Everything about the origins of the universe, the nature of elementary particles and the forces between them.

But that is not actually a Theory of Everything, is it? I mean, it doesn't explain *everything*!

Professor Ervin Laszlo, a Hungarian philosopher of science, systems theorist and integral theorist, says that:

the basic concept – the veritable kingpin – of genuine unified theories is universal interconnection. Indeed, the very possibility of such a theory hinges on finding the field in the universe that would connect atoms and galaxies, mice and men, brains and minds, and feed back information from each to all, and from all to each.

There are many paradoxes observed from all of the sciences (physical, biological, psychological and even sociological) that simply cannot be explained unless there is some subtle interconnection. Only a universal field of some sort, an interconnecting field could explain these paradoxes. But just what could it be and where could it exist?

For countless years it has been thought that space was just that, nothingness, a vacuum. Science has discovered that it is not that at all. It is in fact a **plenum**, which means that it is a filled space, or that it contains something. Scientists now talk about it as the **quantum vacuum**.

Space, Ervin Laszlo tells us, is filled with an intense energy that is known as the 'zero-point field' (ZPF). Beyond or underlying this he postulates that there is a fundamental field of which the ZPF is a manifestation. This fundamental field is informational and records everything that has ever happened within it, and it is absolutely interconnecting. Everything in existence is connected to it and by it.

Professor Laszlo has spent more than 40 years exploring and investigating this concept. In a series of books, culminating in *Science and the Akashic Field*, he has developed the idea of the fundamental field, which he calls the Akashic or A-field.

Perhaps it is the direction in which we should be looking to discover that elusive Integral Theory of Everything.

The challenge ahead

I am certainly not bright enough to add to this debate. I can merely look at the achievements of these great scientists and let out a sigh of awe. In this book of my schooldays' science remembered and the home experiments that I did, I hope that I may have persuaded (or reminded) you that science really is cool.

Now perhaps you will feel stimulated to go out and discover the Theory of Everything yourself. Good luck!

TIMELINE OF THE HISTORY OF SCIENCE

This timeline is a list of approximate dates for many of the experiments, discoveries or publication of papers and books that are mentioned in these pages (or which should have been). My apologies for any glaring omissions of history that I have made.

c8,000BC	Vinegar first discovered and used
c4,000BC	Egyptians start making bread
c3,300BC	Egyptians begin mummification of their dead
c3,000BC	A medical papyrus from Egypt indicates that vinegar is useful as an antiseptic
c2,600BC	Flush toilets a regular feature in homes in the Indian cities of Harappa and Mohendaro
c1,700BC	Westcar Papyrus details magic and conjuring from the days of King Khufu
c1550BC	Ebers Papyrus, a treatise on medical treatments, is written
c1550BC	Edwin Smith Papyrus, a treatise on surgery, is written
c600BC	Thales of Miletus discovers the phenomenon that came to be known as static electricity
c460BC	Empedocles (490–430BC) proposes that everything is made up of four elements – earth, air, fire and water
c430BC	Democritus (460–370BC) proposes the first Atomic Theory
c400BC	Hippocrates, the Father of Medicine, writes the Hippocratic Oath
c360BC	Plato (428–348BC) first uses the term 'element'
c350BC	Aristotle (384–322BC) works in several areas of science and medicine. He was the first effective anatomist
c300BC	The great Library of Alexandria established
c250BC	Archimedes (287–212BC) active and invents the Archimedean screw, the lever and famously has his Eureka moment

AD47	Aulus Cornelius Celsus (25BC–AD50) writes *de Medicina*, a great treatise on anatomy and medicine
c50	Hero of Alexandria invents the *aelilophile*, a type of steam engine, and the first coin-operated vending machine
79	Mount Vesuvius erupts to engulf the cities of Herculaneum and Pompeii
c160	Galen (AD131–201) makes extensive anatomical dissections and names many of the anatomical structures that we recognize today
1070s	The Bayeux Tapestry shows a sighting of Halley's Comet
c1520	Paracelsus (1493–1541) discovers zinc
1543	Andreas Vesalius (1514–1564) publishes the first anatomically accurate medical textbook, *De Humani Corporis Fabrica*
c1590	Dr Thomas Muffet (1553–1604) publishes *Health Improvement*
1600	Dr William Gilbert (1544–1603) conducts the first experiments on magnetism and shows that the earth behaves like a giant magnet
1609	Galileo Galilei makes the first use of his astronomical telescope
1616	William Harvey (1578–1657) demonstrates the circulation of the blood
1620	Sir Francis Bacon (1561–1626) publishes *Novum Organum*, a treatise on logic and the scientific method, in which he advocates experimentation. He died from pneumonia after catching a cold when stuffing a chicken with snow in an early experiment on refrigeration
1637	René Descartes (1596–1650) writes *Discourse on the Method*, setting out his philosophy summed up by the expression '*Cogito ergo sum*' – 'I think, therefore I am.' This heralded the beginning of 'Cartesian dualism'
1658	Johann Rudolph Glauber (1604–1670) discovers acid–alkali reactions and salt formation
1661	Robert Boyle (1627–1691) writes *The Sceptical Chemyst* and later proposes Boyle's Law
1664	Robert Boyle publishes *Experimental History of Colours* in which he demonstrates the use of indicators. He later introduces litmus paper
c1665	Marcello Malpighi (1628–1694) discovers capillaries in the lung of a frog
c1665	Thomas Willis (1621–1675) describes the Circle of Willis, the blood supply to the brain

1665	Robert Hooke (1635–1703) publishes *Micrographia*
1666	The Great Fire of London
1669	Hennig Brand (1630–1710) discovers the element phosphorus
1680	Robert Boyle (1627–1691) invents the match
1681	Denis Papin invents the pressure cooker
1687	Sir Isaac Newton publishes *Philosophia Naturalis Mathematica Principia* (*Mathematical Principles of Natural Philosophy*)
1698	Thomas Savery builds the first steam pump
1703	George Stahl (1660–1734) proposes the phlogiston theory to explain what happens when substances are burned, or when metals like iron rust
1704	Sir Isaac Newton publishes *Opticks*
1705	Edmond Halley (1656–1742) predicts that a comet would reappear in 1758. It did and it was named after him
1738	Daniel Bernoulli (1700–1782) publishes his book *Hydrodynamica*, which introduces the Bernoulli Principle
1749	John Hunter (1728–1793) begins to work as an assistant to his brother William at his School of Anatomy in Covent Garden in London
1752	Benjamin Franklin (1706–1790) performs his famous electric kite experiment, proving that lightning is caused by an electrical discharge
c1755	Joseph Black (1728–1799) discovers carbon dioxide
1761	Pieter van Musschenbroek (1692–1761) invents the Leiden jar, the first capacitor
1774	Joseph Priestley (1733–1804) discovers oxygen – although he called it dephlogisticated air
1776	Henry Cavendish (1731–1810) discovers hydrogen, which he calls inflammable air
1779	Antoine-Laurent de Lavoisier (1743–1794) renames Priestley's dephlogisticated air oxygen
1782	James Watt invents the first rotary steam engine
1783	Antoine-Laurent de Lavoisier (1743–1794) finally disproves the phlogiston theory
1791	Luigi Galvani (1737–1798), while conducting experiments on animal electricity, notices that dead frogs' muscles twitch when in contact with brass and iron
1799	Alessandro Volta (1745–1827) invents the Voltaic pile, the first effective battery
1803	John Dalton (1766–1844) proposes his atomic theory

1808	Jöns Jacob Berzelius (1779–1848) proposes the use of chemical formulae
1809	Dr Leopold Auenbrugger (1722–1809) introduces his science of percussion to medicine. His book *Novum Inventum* is not published until 1851
1815	Sir Humphry Davy invents the Davy lamp
1816	René Théophile Hyacinthe Laennec (1781–1826) invents the stethoscope
1820	Hans Christian Ørsted (1777–1851) discovers the electromagnetic field
1827	Robert Brown (1773–1858) describes Brownian motion when observing pollen grains and moss spores
1829	George Stephenson builds his Rocket, the first effective locomotive
1830	Joseph Jackson Lister (1786–1869) invents the compound microscope
1831	Charles Darwin (1809–1882) embarks on the second voyage of HMS *Beagle*
1827	Robert Brown (1773–1858) describes the cell nucleus when studying cells from orchids
1851	Dr Leopold Auenbrugger (1722–1809) publishes *Novum Inventum*, in which he introduces his science of percussion to medicine
1852	Dr George Cammann invents the first two-ear-piece stethoscope
1858	August Ferdinand Möbius (1790–1868) describes the Möbius band
1859	Charles Darwin (1809–1882) publishes *On the Origin of the Species*
1860	The first public flushing toilets are installed at the Crystal Palace. The charge to use them was one penny, hence the expression 'to spend a penny'
1865	Friedrich August Kekulé describes the structure of benzene
1869	Dmitri Ivanovich Mendeleev (1834–1907) publishes his Periodic Table of the Elements
1876	Alexander Graham Bell (1847–1922) invents the telephone
1879	Constantin Fahlberg (1850–1910) discovers saccharin
1884	Henry Louis Le Chatelier (1850–1936) proposes Le Chatelier Principle of chemical equilibrium
1896	Guglielmo Marconi (1874–1937) makes his first radio transmissions
1901	Wilhelm Conrad Röntgen (1845–1923) is awarded the first

	Nobel Prize for Physics for his discovery of Röntgen or X-rays
1909	Søren Peder Lauritz Sørensen proposes the pH scale of acidity and alkalinity
1909	Guglielmo Marconi is awarded the Nobel Prize for physics
1912	Louis Camille Maillaird describes the Maillard Reaction, one of the basic principles involved in cooking chemistry
1915	Albert Einstein (1879–1955) publishes his theory of general relativity
1921	Einstein receives the Nobel Prize for his work on theoretical physics and the discovery of the photoelectric effect
1922	Niels Henrik David Bohr (1885–1962), one of the great minds in quantum mechanics, receives the Nobel Prize for his services in the investigation of the structure of atoms and of the radiation emanating from them
1931	Max Knoll (1897–1969) and Ernst Ruska (1906–1988) invent the electron microscope
1932	Frits Zernike (1888–1966) invents the phase-contrast microscope
1945	Alexander Fleming (1881–1955), Howard Walter Florey (1898–1968) and Ernst Boris Chain (1906–1979) jointly awarded the Nobel Prize for Medicine and Physiology for the discovery of penicillin
1953	James Watson (1928–) and Francis Crick (1916–2004) discover the structure of DNA
1962	James Watson and Francis Crick awarded the Nobel Prize for Medicine for their work on nucleic acids
1979	Sheldon Lee Glashow (1932–), Steven Weinberg (1933–) and Abdus Salam (1926–1996) win the Nobel Prize for Physics for showing that the weak nuclear force and the electromagnetic force are manifestations of a single force, called the electroweak force
1996	Ervin Laszlo (1932–) postulates the existence of an all-pervading informational field, the A-field
2002	The fictional detective Sherlock Holmes is awarded an 'Extraordinary Honorary Fellowship' in London by the Royal Society for Chemistry
2008	The Large Hadron Collider (LHC), the world's largest and highest-energy particle accelerator, is first operated at Cern in Switzerland

NOTES

1   Atmospheric pressure has been measured in a variety of units. The following are all equivalent. You will recognize one according to when your schooldays were! 101.3 kPa (kilo Pascals), 1013 mb (millibars), 760 mmHg (millimetres of mercury) or 14.6 PSI (pounds per square inch).

2   The freezing point of water is the same as the melting point of ice.

3   People with the condition of coeliac disease are sensitive to gluten in the diet. They should not consume bread made in this way.

4   The atomic number indicates the number of protons in each atom of the element. The higher the number, the heavier the element, with hydrogen at atomic number 1 being the lightest and lead at atomic number 82 being one of the heaviest.

5   Benzene was actually first discovered by Michael Faraday.

6   Robert F Curl Jr, Sir Harold Kroto and Richard E Smalley were awarded the 1996 Nobel Prize for Chemistry for their discovery of fullerenes.

7   In the fermentation of ethyl alcohol acetic acid is the main acid produced, but there will also be some tartaric acid and citric acid.

8   Lichens are composite organisms – a fungus and an alga or a cyanobacterium – living in symbiotic (mutually beneficial) relationship to each other.

9   Scurvy is a condition caused by vitamin C deficiency. It causes bruising, bleeding from the gums and mucus membranes so that serious anaemia may be caused. It was a real problem for sailors on long sea voyages until James Lind discovered that it could be treated with citrus fruits. He wrote about it in a book entitled *A Treatise of the Scurvy* in 1753.

10 Henry Cavendish (1731–1810) discovered hydrogen, but is also noted for his work on electricity and the famous Cavendish Experiment, when he measured the weight or the density of the earth.

11 Sir Isaac Newton and Gottfried Leibniz (1646–1716) both have a claim on the invention of calculus. Newton referred to his as the 'method of fluxions' and the 'inverse method of fluxions' (from the

Latin, meaning 'flow'. Leibniz called his method differential and integral calculus. Newton is regarded as being the first to arrive at his method, but Leibniz undoubtedly arrived at his method independently. It is Leibniz's terms that have survived – thankfully!

12   Melanins are pigmented compounds present in plant and animal tissues. They cause browning in fruits and freckles and moles in human beings.

13   In 1901 Albert Einstein published the first of over 300 scientific papers that he would write between then and 1954. This first was *Conclusions Drawn from the Phenomena of Capillarity*. In 1905 he started to publish his groundbreaking works on relativity.

14   Daniel Bernoulli (1700–1782) was a Dutch–Swiss mathematician who described the Bernoulli Principle. Essentially, as the velocity of a fluid increases, so the pressure exerted by that fluid is reduced. It is partly this that provides aircraft with their lift.

15   The word telescope was coined by the Greek mathematician Giovanni Demisiani in 1611, after Galileo Galilei presented the Lincean Academy, the first scientific academy in Italy, with one of his instruments. The word comes from the Greek words *tele*, meaning 'far' and *skopein*, meaning 'to look at.'

16   Pluto was for many years considered to be a planet, but there has long been controversy as to whether it should just be classified as a comet. It was decided in 2006 that it should be regarded as a dwarf planet.

17   Halley's Comet, named after Edmond Halley (1656-1742), astronomer, mathematician and physicist.

18   The Leiden jar was invented by Pieter van Musschenbroek (1692–1761), a professor of mathematics and medicine at Leiden University, in 1761. The apparatus consisted of a jar with a covering and a lining of metal, capable of storing a charge of static electricity. It was a form of early capacitor. Its great disadvantage was that the charge could not be controlled, so that once discharged, it discharged totally.

19   LED – light emitting diode. A diode is an electronics component that only permits electricity to flow in one direction. A light emitting diode does the same thing, but gives off light when electricity passes in the right direction through it. It needs less electricity than an electric bulb so is good if you are only using weak currents, such as here.

20   If you want to enjoy building a Foxhole radio set, but be sure that it works, then you can obtain a very reasonably priced kit containing instructions and all that you need from the very helpful Lance Borden, at: Lance S Borden, WB5REX, Borden Radio Company, 13911 Kensington Place, Houston, Texas 77034 (www.xtalman.com).

21   Jejunum means 'empty', because Galen found this always to be empty

in animal specimens. This is actually a post-mortem finding, since it is full in life.

22 Rectum means 'straight' because Galen always found it to be straight in animals.

23 Radius means 'spoke', because Galen thought it looked similar to the spoke of a chariot wheel.

24 There are twelve cranial nerves on each side of the head. They are nerves that come directly from the brain stem, as opposed to spinal nerves, which supply the rest of the body, and which come from the spinal cord.

25 Möbius bands are chiral – that is, they have handedness, as in right and left handedness.

26 The Emperor Claudius (Tiberius Claudius Drusus Nero Germanicus, 10BC–AD54), nephew of Tiberius, uncle of Caligula, the conqueror of Britain in AD43, was an appointed augur. Augurs were respected Roman officials. Their function was to read omens and portents from which auspices could be taken. They read the weather, the flight of birds, the feeding of the sacred chickens, the behaviour of four-footed animals and the movement of finger rings – dactylomancy.

INDEX